50 Canadian Food Recipes for Home

By: Kelly Johnson

Table of Contents

- Poutine
- Butter Tarts
- Tourtière
- Nanaimo Bars
- Peameal Bacon Sandwich
- Beef Stroganoff
- Maple Glazed Salmon
- Bannock
- Caesar Cocktail
- Tourtière de Maman
- Pancakes with Maple Syrup
- Montreal Smoked Meat
- Split Pea Soup
- Maple Bacon Doughnuts
- Cedar-Plank Salmon
- Cornish Pasties
- Wild Blueberry Pie
- Nova Scotia Lobster Roll
- Saskatoon Berry Jam
- Maple Syrup Pie
- Crispy Samosas
- Caribou Stew
- Ketchup Chips
- Yellow Pea Soup
- Liver and Onions
- Canadian Bacon and Eggs
- Salmon Gravlax
- Cedar Plank Grilled Trout
- Roasted Root Vegetables
- Squash Soup
- Bison Burger
- Sweet Corn Fritters

- Pork Tenderloin with Apples
- Maple-Glazed Carrots
- Cinnamon Buns
- Apple Crisp
- Beef Pot Roast
- Turkey with Cranberry Sauce
- Fish Tacos
- Maple Mustard Pork Chops
- Scalloped Potatoes
- Blackberry Crisp
- Gingerbread Cookies
- Maple Walnut Granola
- Rhubarb Pie
- Sour Cherry Soup
- BBQ Ribs
- Vegetarian Shepherd's Pie
- Lemon Curd Tarts
- Sweet Potato Fries

Butter Tarts

Ingredients:

For the pastry:

- 2 1/2 cups all-purpose flour
- 1/2 cup granulated sugar
- 1 cup unsalted butter, cold and cut into small pieces
- 1 large egg yolk
- 2-3 tablespoons cold water

For the filling:

- 1 cup unsalted butter
- 1 cup brown sugar
- 2 large eggs
- 1 tablespoon vanilla extract
- 2 tablespoons all-purpose flour
- A pinch of salt
- Optional: 1/2 cup chopped nuts (like pecans or walnuts) or raisins

Instructions:

1. **Prepare the Pastry:**
    1. In a large bowl, combine the flour and sugar.
    2. Cut in the cold butter using a pastry cutter or your fingers until the mixture resembles coarse crumbs.
    3. Add the egg yolk and mix gently.
    4. Gradually add cold water, one tablespoon at a time, until the dough just comes together.
    5. Divide the dough into two discs, wrap in plastic wrap, and refrigerate for at least 30 minutes.
2. **Prepare the Filling:**
    1. In a medium saucepan, melt the butter over low heat.
    2. Stir in the brown sugar until fully dissolved and smooth.
    3. Remove from heat and let it cool slightly.
    4. Whisk in the eggs, one at a time, then add the vanilla extract.
    5. Stir in the flour and salt until the mixture is well combined.
3. **Assemble the Tarts:**
    1. Preheat your oven to 375°F (190°C).
    2. On a floured surface, roll out one disc of dough to about 1/8 inch thickness. Cut out circles that fit into your muffin tin.
    3. Press the dough circles into the muffin tin wells, trimming off any excess.

4. If using nuts or raisins, place a small amount in the bottom of each pastry shell.
5. Spoon the filling mixture into each shell, filling about 3/4 full.

4. **Bake:**
    1. Bake in the preheated oven for 15-20 minutes, or until the filling is set and the pastry is golden brown.
    2. Allow the tarts to cool completely in the tin before removing.

Enjoy your homemade butter tarts with a cup of tea or coffee! They're perfect for sharing or indulging in a sweet treat.

Tourtière

Ingredients:

For the filling:

- 1 lb (450g) ground pork
- 1/2 lb (225g) ground beef
- 1 small onion, finely chopped
- 2 cloves garlic, minced
- 1 medium potato, peeled and grated
- 1/2 cup beef broth
- 1 teaspoon ground cinnamon
- 1/2 teaspoon ground cloves
- 1/2 teaspoon dried thyme
- 1/2 teaspoon ground allspice
- Salt and black pepper to taste
- 2 tablespoons vegetable oil

For the pastry:

- 2 1/2 cups all-purpose flour
- 1 teaspoon salt
- 1 cup unsalted butter, cold and cut into small pieces
- 6-8 tablespoons ice water

Instructions:

1. **Prepare the Pastry:**
    1. In a large bowl, combine the flour and salt.
    2. Cut in the cold butter using a pastry cutter or your fingers until the mixture resembles coarse crumbs.
    3. Gradually add ice water, one tablespoon at a time, until the dough just comes together.
    4. Divide the dough into two discs, wrap in plastic wrap, and refrigerate for at least 30 minutes.
2. **Prepare the Filling:**
    1. In a large skillet, heat the vegetable oil over medium heat.
    2. Add the chopped onion and garlic and cook until softened.
    3. Add the ground pork and beef, and cook until browned, breaking up the meat with a spoon.
    4. Stir in the grated potato, beef broth, cinnamon, cloves, thyme, allspice, salt, and pepper.

5. Simmer the mixture for about 10-15 minutes, or until the potato is tender and the mixture is thickened. Let it cool slightly.

3. **Assemble the Tourtière:**
    1. Preheat your oven to 375°F (190°C).
    2. Roll out one disc of dough on a floured surface to fit your pie dish. Transfer the dough to the dish and trim the edges.
    3. Spoon the meat filling into the pastry-lined dish.
    4. Roll out the second disc of dough and place it over the filling. Trim, seal, and crimp the edges.
    5. Cut a few small slits in the top crust to allow steam to escape.
4. **Bake:**
    1. Bake in the preheated oven for 45-55 minutes, or until the crust is golden brown and the filling is bubbling.
    2. Let the pie cool for a few minutes before serving.

Tourtière is often enjoyed with a side of ketchup, mustard, or pickles. It's a hearty and comforting dish that's perfect for special occasions or a cozy family dinner.

Nanaimo Bars

Ingredients:

For the base:

- 1/2 cup unsalted butter, melted
- 2 cups graham cracker crumbs
- 1 cup shredded coconut
- 1 cup chopped walnuts or pecans (optional, can be omitted)

For the custard layer:

- 1/2 cup unsalted butter, softened
- 2 cups powdered sugar
- 2 tablespoons vanilla custard powder (not instant pudding)
- 2 tablespoons milk

For the chocolate topping:

- 4 ounces (115g) semi-sweet chocolate, chopped
- 2 tablespoons unsalted butter

Instructions:

1. **Prepare the Base:**
    1. In a medium bowl, combine the melted butter, graham cracker crumbs, shredded coconut, and nuts (if using). Mix until well combined.
    2. Press the mixture firmly into the bottom of a greased 9x9-inch (23x23 cm) baking pan to create an even layer. Chill in the refrigerator while you prepare the next layer.
2. **Prepare the Custard Layer:**
    1. In a medium bowl, beat the softened butter until creamy.
    2. Gradually add the powdered sugar, custard powder, and milk. Beat until smooth and well combined.
    3. Spread the custard mixture evenly over the chilled base layer. Smooth it out with a spatula and return to the refrigerator to chill while you prepare the topping.
3. **Prepare the Chocolate Topping:**
    1. In a heatproof bowl set over a pot of simmering water (double boiler), melt the chocolate and butter together, stirring until smooth and fully combined.
    2. Pour the chocolate mixture over the custard layer and spread it evenly.
4. **Chill and Cut:**
    1. Refrigerate the bars for at least 2 hours, or until the chocolate is set and the bars are firm.

2. Once chilled, cut into squares or rectangles.

Nanaimo Bars are best stored in the refrigerator to keep their texture, but they can also be frozen if you want to make them ahead of time. Enjoy these rich, layered treats with a cup of coffee or tea!

Peameal Bacon Sandwich

Ingredients:

- **For the Peameal Bacon:**
    - 1 lb (450g) peameal bacon (also known as back bacon)
    - 1 tablespoon vegetable oil
- **For the Sandwich:**
    - 4 sandwich rolls or buns (such as kaiser rolls or brioche)
    - 4 tablespoons mustard (Dijon or yellow, as per preference)
    - Lettuce leaves
    - Tomato slices
    - Pickles (optional)
    - Other optional toppings: cheese, onions, or a fried egg

Instructions:

1. **Prepare the Peameal Bacon:**
    1. If the peameal bacon is not pre-sliced, slice it into 1/2-inch (1.3 cm) thick pieces.
    2. Heat the vegetable oil in a large skillet over medium heat.
    3. Cook the peameal bacon slices in the skillet, turning occasionally, until they are browned and crispy on both sides. This usually takes about 4-5 minutes per side.
    4. Transfer the cooked bacon to a paper towel-lined plate to drain any excess oil.
2. **Prepare the Sandwich Rolls:**
    1. While the bacon is cooking, you can lightly toast the sandwich rolls if desired. To do this, place them cut-side down on a skillet or under a broiler until they are golden brown.
3. **Assemble the Sandwich:**
    1. Spread a tablespoon of mustard on the bottom half of each roll.
    2. Place a few slices of cooked peameal bacon on top of the mustard.
    3. Add lettuce leaves and tomato slices over the bacon.
    4. Top with pickles or any other desired toppings.
    5. Place the top half of the roll on the sandwich and press down gently.
4. **Serve:**
    1. Serve the sandwiches immediately while the bacon is still warm.

Peameal Bacon Sandwiches are simple yet flavorful, offering a nice balance of savory, tangy, and fresh elements. Enjoy them as part of a hearty breakfast or a satisfying lunch!

Beef Stroganoff

Ingredients:

- **For the Beef:**
    - 1 lb (450g) beef sirloin or tenderloin, sliced into thin strips
    - Salt and black pepper, to taste
    - 2 tablespoons vegetable oil or butter
- **For the Sauce:**
    - 1 medium onion, finely chopped
    - 2 cloves garlic, minced
    - 8 oz (225g) mushrooms, sliced (cremini or button mushrooms work well)
    - 1 cup beef broth
    - 1 tablespoon Dijon mustard
    - 1 tablespoon Worcestershire sauce
    - 1 cup sour cream (or Greek yogurt as a substitute)
    - 1 tablespoon all-purpose flour (optional, for thickening)
    - 2 tablespoons chopped fresh parsley (for garnish)
- **To Serve:**
    - Cooked egg noodles, rice, or mashed potatoes

Instructions:

1. **Prepare the Beef:**
    1. Season the beef strips with salt and black pepper.
    2. Heat the vegetable oil or butter in a large skillet over medium-high heat.
    3. Add the beef strips to the skillet in batches to avoid overcrowding. Sear the beef until browned on all sides but not fully cooked through. Transfer the beef to a plate and set aside.
2. **Prepare the Sauce:**
    1. In the same skillet, add a bit more oil or butter if needed. Add the chopped onion and cook until softened, about 3-4 minutes.
    2. Add the minced garlic and sliced mushrooms. Cook until the mushrooms are browned and have released their moisture, about 5-6 minutes.
    3. Stir in the flour if using, and cook for an additional minute.
    4. Pour in the beef broth, Dijon mustard, and Worcestershire sauce. Stir well to combine and bring to a simmer. Let it cook for about 3-4 minutes, or until the sauce starts to thicken.
3. **Combine and Finish:**
    1. Return the browned beef strips to the skillet. Stir to coat the beef in the sauce and simmer for about 5 minutes, or until the beef is cooked through and tender.

2. Reduce the heat to low and stir in the sour cream. Cook gently until heated through. Adjust seasoning with salt and pepper to taste. If the sauce is too thick, you can add a bit more beef broth to reach your desired consistency.
4. **Serve:**
    1. Serve the Beef Stroganoff over cooked egg noodles, rice, or mashed potatoes.
    2. Garnish with chopped fresh parsley.

Tips:

- **Beef Cuts:** For the best texture, use tender cuts like sirloin or tenderloin. Avoid cooking the beef over high heat for too long, as it can become tough.
- **Sour Cream Substitute:** If you prefer, Greek yogurt can be used as a lower-fat substitute for sour cream.
- **Thickening:** If you like a thicker sauce, you can mix a tablespoon of flour with a small amount of water to make a slurry and stir it into the sauce.

Enjoy this comforting and flavorful Beef Stroganoff with your favorite side!

Maple Glazed Salmon

Ingredients:

- **For the Salmon:**
    - 4 salmon fillets (about 6 oz or 170g each)
    - Salt and black pepper, to taste
    - 1 tablespoon olive oil
- **For the Maple Glaze:**
    - 1/4 cup pure maple syrup
    - 2 tablespoons soy sauce
    - 2 tablespoons Dijon mustard
    - 1 tablespoon lemon juice
    - 1 clove garlic, minced
    - 1 teaspoon grated fresh ginger (optional)
    - 1 teaspoon cornstarch mixed with 1 tablespoon water (optional, for thickening)
- **For Garnish:**
    - Chopped fresh parsley or green onions
    - Lemon wedges

Instructions:

1. **Prepare the Maple Glaze:**
    1. In a small saucepan, combine the maple syrup, soy sauce, Dijon mustard, lemon juice, garlic, and ginger (if using).
    2. Bring the mixture to a simmer over medium heat, stirring occasionally.
    3. If you prefer a thicker glaze, stir in the cornstarch-water mixture and cook for an additional 1-2 minutes until the glaze has thickened. Remove from heat and set aside.
2. **Prepare the Salmon:**
    1. Preheat your oven to 400°F (200°C). Alternatively, you can grill the salmon if you prefer.
    2. Line a baking sheet with parchment paper or lightly grease it with olive oil.
    3. Season the salmon fillets with salt and black pepper. Brush them with olive oil.
3. **Cook the Salmon:**
    1. Place the salmon fillets on the prepared baking sheet.
    2. Brush a generous amount of the maple glaze over each fillet.
    3. Bake in the preheated oven for about 12-15 minutes, or until the salmon is cooked through and flakes easily with a fork. If you like, you can broil the salmon for the last 1-2 minutes to caramelize the glaze slightly.
4. **Serve:**
    1. Transfer the salmon fillets to serving plates.

2. Drizzle with additional maple glaze if desired.
3. Garnish with chopped fresh parsley or green onions and serve with lemon wedges on the side.

Tips:

- **Salmon:** Look for fresh, high-quality salmon fillets. You can use skinless or skin-on fillets based on your preference.
- **Glaze Variations:** Feel free to adjust the sweetness or saltiness of the glaze by adding more or less maple syrup or soy sauce.
- **Side Dishes:** Maple Glazed Salmon pairs well with a variety of sides, such as roasted vegetables, rice, quinoa, or a fresh salad.

This dish is not only tasty but also visually appealing, making it a great option for both everyday meals and special occasions. Enjoy!

Bannock

Ingredients:

- 2 cups all-purpose flour
- 2 tablespoons baking powder
- 1/2 teaspoon salt
- 1/4 cup sugar (optional, depending on whether you want a sweet or savory bannock)
- 1/4 cup cold butter or lard, cut into small pieces
- 1 cup milk (or water, if preferred)
- 1 egg (optional, for a richer texture)

Instructions:

1. **Prepare the Dough:**
   - In a large bowl, combine the flour, baking powder, salt, and sugar (if using).
   - Cut in the cold butter or lard using a pastry cutter or your fingers until the mixture resembles coarse crumbs.
   - If using, beat the egg and add it to the milk. Pour this mixture into the dry ingredients.
   - Stir until the dough just comes together. Be careful not to overmix; it's okay if there are a few lumps.
2. **Cook the Bannock:**
   Baked Bannock:
   - Preheat your oven to 400°F (200°C).
   - Transfer the dough to a lightly floured surface and shape it into a round or rectangle, about 1 inch thick.
   - Place the dough on a baking sheet lined with parchment paper or lightly greased.
   - Bake for about 20-25 minutes, or until the bannock is golden brown and sounds hollow when tapped on the bottom.
3. **Fried Bannock:**
   - Heat a few tablespoons of oil in a large skillet over medium heat.
   - Divide the dough into smaller portions or shape it into flat rounds.
   - Fry each piece for about 3-4 minutes per side, or until golden brown and cooked through.
4. **Campfire Bannock:**
   - Shape the dough into a flat round or wrap it around a stick.
   - Cook over a campfire or grill, turning frequently, until it's golden brown and cooked through.
5. **Serve:**
   - Serve the bannock warm, with butter, jam, honey, or your favorite toppings. It's also great alongside soups and stews.

Tips:

- **Variations:** You can customize bannock by adding ingredients like cheese, herbs, or dried fruits to the dough before cooking.
- **Texture:** For a softer, fluffier texture, use milk. For a denser bread, you can use water.
- **Storage:** Bannock is best enjoyed fresh but can be stored in an airtight container at room temperature for a few days or frozen for longer storage.

Bannock is a versatile bread that adapts well to different cooking methods and flavors, making it a staple in many households. Enjoy experimenting with it!

Caesar Cocktail

Ingredients:

- **For the Rim:**
    - 1 lemon wedge
    - 1/4 cup celery salt or a mixture of celery salt and coarse salt
- **For the Cocktail:**
    - 1 1/2 oz vodka
    - 4 oz Clamato juice (or a tomato juice substitute if you can't find Clamato)
    - 1 dash hot sauce (e.g., Tabasco)
    - 1 dash Worcestershire sauce
    - 1/4 teaspoon prepared horseradish (optional, for extra kick)
    - Freshly ground black pepper, to taste
- **For Garnish:**
    - Celery stalk
    - Lemon wedge
    - Pickles or olives (optional)
    - Cooked shrimp or bacon strip (optional, for a more elaborate garnish)

Instructions:

1. **Prepare the Glass:**
    1. Moisten the rim of a tall glass (like a pint glass) with the lemon wedge.
    2. Dip the rim into the celery salt or salt mixture to coat it. Set the glass aside.
2. **Mix the Cocktail:**
    1. In a shaker or directly in the prepared glass, combine the vodka, Clamato juice, hot sauce, Worcestershire sauce, and prepared horseradish (if using).
    2. Stir gently to mix. Avoid shaking, as this can create too much foam and dilute the drink.
3. **Season and Serve:**
    1. Add freshly ground black pepper to taste.
    2. Fill the glass with ice cubes.
    3. Pour the cocktail mixture over the ice.
4. **Garnish:**
    1. Garnish with a celery stalk, lemon wedge, and any additional garnishes like pickles, olives, or a shrimp.

Tips:

- **Clamato Juice:** If Clamato juice is not available, you can use a mix of tomato juice and clam juice, or just tomato juice with extra seasoning.

- **Spice Level:** Adjust the amount of hot sauce and horseradish according to your preference for spiciness.
- **Garnishes:** Get creative with garnishes; a strip of crispy bacon, a skewer of olives, or even a skewer with a shrimp can make the drink more festive.

The Caesar is a beloved cocktail known for its bold flavors and versatility, making it a great choice for a variety of occasions. Enjoy!

Tourtière de Maman

Ingredients:

For the Pie Crust:

- 2 1/2 cups all-purpose flour
- 1/2 teaspoon salt
- 1 cup unsalted butter, cold and cut into small cubes
- 6-8 tablespoons ice water

For the Filling:

- 1 lb (450g) ground pork
- 1/2 lb (225g) ground beef
- 1/2 lb (225g) ground veal (or more pork or beef if veal is unavailable)
- 1 medium onion, finely chopped
- 2 cloves garlic, minced
- 1 small potato, peeled and grated
- 1/2 cup beef broth
- 1 teaspoon ground cinnamon
- 1/2 teaspoon ground cloves
- 1/2 teaspoon dried thyme
- 1/2 teaspoon ground allspice
- Salt and black pepper to taste

For Assembly:

- 1 egg, beaten (for egg wash)

Instructions:

1. **Prepare the Pie Crust:**
    1. In a large bowl, mix the flour and salt.
    2. Cut in the cold butter using a pastry cutter or your fingers until the mixture resembles coarse crumbs.
    3. Gradually add ice water, one tablespoon at a time, until the dough just comes together. Be careful not to overwork the dough.
    4. Divide the dough into two equal portions, shape into discs, wrap in plastic wrap, and refrigerate for at least 30 minutes.
2. **Prepare the Filling:**
    1. In a large skillet or saucepan, cook the ground meats over medium heat until browned, breaking them up with a spoon. Drain excess fat if necessary.

2. Add the chopped onion and minced garlic, cooking until softened.
3. Stir in the grated potato, beef broth, cinnamon, cloves, thyme, allspice, salt, and pepper.
4. Simmer the mixture for about 10-15 minutes, or until the potato is tender and the mixture is thickened. Allow it to cool slightly.

3. **Assemble the Tourtière:**
   1. Preheat your oven to 375°F (190°C).
   2. Roll out one disc of dough on a floured surface to fit your pie dish. Transfer the dough to the dish and trim the edges.
   3. Spoon the meat filling into the pastry-lined dish, spreading it out evenly.
   4. Roll out the second disc of dough and place it over the filling. Trim, seal, and crimp the edges. Cut a few small slits in the top crust to allow steam to escape.
   5. Brush the top crust with the beaten egg for a golden finish.

4. **Bake:**
   1. Bake in the preheated oven for 45-55 minutes, or until the crust is golden brown and the filling is bubbling.
   2. Let the pie cool for at least 10 minutes before serving.

Tips:

- **Meat Variations:** While pork, beef, and veal are traditional, you can adjust the meat mixture according to your preferences or availability.
- **Seasoning:** Adjust the spices to taste; some people like more cinnamon or cloves for a stronger flavor.
- **Make-Ahead:** Tourtière can be made ahead and frozen. Bake it from frozen, adding a bit more time to ensure it's heated through.

Tourtière de Maman is a heartwarming dish that captures the essence of Quebecois comfort food, making it a perfect centerpiece for festive meals or family gatherings. Enjoy!

Pancakes with Maple Syrup

Ingredients:

For the Pancakes:

- 1 1/2 cups all-purpose flour
- 2 tablespoons granulated sugar
- 1 tablespoon baking powder
- 1/2 teaspoon salt
- 1 1/4 cups milk (whole or 2% for best results)
- 1 large egg
- 3 tablespoons unsalted butter, melted
- 1 teaspoon vanilla extract (optional)

For Serving:

- Pure maple syrup
- Fresh fruit, butter, or whipped cream (optional)

Instructions:

1. **Prepare the Batter:**
    1. In a large bowl, whisk together the flour, sugar, baking powder, and salt.
    2. In another bowl, combine the milk, egg, melted butter, and vanilla extract (if using).
    3. Pour the wet ingredients into the dry ingredients and gently stir until just combined. The batter should be slightly lumpy; do not overmix.
2. **Cook the Pancakes:**
    1. Heat a non-stick skillet or griddle over medium heat. Lightly grease with butter or oil.
    2. Pour 1/4 cup of batter onto the skillet for each pancake. Cook until bubbles form on the surface and the edges start to look set, about 2-3 minutes.
    3. Flip the pancake and cook for an additional 1-2 minutes, or until golden brown and cooked through.
    4. Repeat with the remaining batter, adding more butter or oil to the skillet as needed.
3. **Serve:**
    1. Serve the pancakes warm, stacked on a plate.
    2. Drizzle with pure maple syrup and add any additional toppings you like, such as fresh fruit, a pat of butter, or whipped cream.

Tips:

- **Batter Consistency:** If the batter is too thick, you can add a little more milk to reach your desired consistency. If it's too thin, add a bit more flour.
- **Heat Control:** If your pancakes are browning too quickly, reduce the heat slightly to ensure they cook evenly.
- **Keep Warm:** To keep pancakes warm while you cook the rest, place them in a single layer on a baking sheet in a preheated oven at 200°F (93°C).

Enjoy your homemade pancakes with pure maple syrup and any additional toppings you love!

Montreal Smoked Meat

Ingredients:

For the Brine:

- 4 cups water
- 1/2 cup kosher salt
- 1/4 cup sugar
- 1 tablespoon Prague Powder #1 (curing salt; optional but helps with preservation and color)
- 2 tablespoons black peppercorns
- 1 tablespoon coriander seeds
- 1 tablespoon mustard seeds
- 4 cloves garlic, minced
- 1 tablespoon paprika
- 1 tablespoon cracked black pepper (for rub)
- 1 tablespoon ground coriander (for rub)

For the Rub:

- 2 tablespoons black pepper
- 1 tablespoon ground coriander

For Cooking:

- 1 beef brisket (about 4-5 lbs or 1.8-2.3 kg)

Instructions:

1. **Prepare the Brine:**
    1. In a large pot, combine the water, kosher salt, sugar, Prague Powder #1 (if using), black peppercorns, coriander seeds, mustard seeds, minced garlic, and paprika.
    2. Heat the mixture over medium heat, stirring until the salt and sugar dissolve completely. Allow it to cool to room temperature.
2. **Brine the Meat:**
    1. Place the brisket in a large, food-safe container or a heavy-duty plastic bag.
    2. Pour the cooled brine over the brisket, making sure it is fully submerged. You can use a weighted plate or a sealed bag to keep the meat submerged.
    3. Refrigerate the meat in the brine for 5-7 days, turning occasionally.
3. **Apply the Rub:**
    1. After brining, remove the brisket from the brine and pat it dry with paper towels.

2. Mix the black pepper and ground coriander together to create the rub.
   3. Coat the brisket evenly with the rub mixture, pressing it in to adhere.
4. **Cook the Meat:**
   1. Preheat your oven to 225°F (107°C).
   2. Place the brisket on a rack in a roasting pan. Cook it in the preheated oven for 4-6 hours, or until it reaches an internal temperature of 190°F (88°C). The meat should be tender and sliceable.
5. **Cool and Slice:**
   1. Once cooked, let the brisket cool to room temperature.
   2. Slice it thinly against the grain. Montreal Smoked Meat is best served warm or at room temperature.
6. **Serve:**
   1. Serve the Montreal Smoked Meat on rye bread with mustard. It's often accompanied by pickles and sometimes coleslaw.

Tips:

- **Curing Salt:** Prague Powder #1 (curing salt) helps in the curing process and improves the color and flavor. It's optional but recommended for authenticity.
- **Smoking:** Traditional Montreal Smoked Meat is smoked after the brining process. If you have access to a smoker, you can smoke the meat at a low temperature for a few hours before cooking it to enhance the flavor.
- **Slicing:** For the best texture, slice the meat thinly against the grain.

Montreal Smoked Meat is a beloved delicacy with its rich, spiced flavor and tender texture, making it a delightful addition to any meal. Enjoy!

Split Pea Soup

Ingredients:

- **For the Soup:**
    - 1 pound (450g) dried green or yellow split peas, rinsed and picked over
    - 1 ham hock or 2 cups diced ham (for a vegetarian option, use vegetable broth and smoked paprika)
    - 1 medium onion, chopped
    - 2 cloves garlic, minced
    - 3 medium carrots, peeled and diced
    - 3 celery stalks, diced
    - 1 bay leaf
    - 1 teaspoon dried thyme
    - 1 teaspoon smoked paprika (optional, for extra smoky flavor)
    - 6 cups low-sodium chicken broth or vegetable broth
    - Salt and black pepper to taste
    - 2 tablespoons olive oil or butter
- **For Garnish (optional):**
    - Fresh parsley, chopped
    - Croutons or bread

Instructions:

1. **Prepare the Ingredients:**
    1. Rinse the split peas under cold water and pick through them to remove any debris.
    2. If using a ham hock, you can soak it in water for a few hours to help remove excess salt if it's a salted version.
2. **Cook the Soup:**
    1. In a large pot or Dutch oven, heat the olive oil or butter over medium heat.
    2. Add the chopped onion and cook until softened, about 5 minutes.
    3. Stir in the minced garlic, diced carrots, and diced celery. Cook for another 5 minutes, until the vegetables begin to soften.
    4. Add the rinsed split peas, ham hock (or diced ham), bay leaf, dried thyme, and smoked paprika (if using). Stir to combine.
    5. Pour in the chicken or vegetable broth. Bring the mixture to a boil.
    6. Reduce the heat to low, cover, and simmer for 1-1.5 hours, or until the split peas are tender and the soup has thickened. If using a ham hock, remove it from the pot after about 1 hour, shred the meat, and return it to the pot. Discard the bone and any excess fat.
3. **Season and Blend (Optional):**

1. Once the split peas are tender, you can use an immersion blender to blend the soup to your desired consistency. For a smoother texture, blend the soup until it's completely smooth. For a chunkier texture, blend just a portion of the soup or leave it as is.
   2. Season the soup with salt and black pepper to taste.
4. **Serve:**
   1. Ladle the soup into bowls and garnish with fresh parsley if desired.
   2. Serve with croutons or crusty bread on the side.

Tips:

- **Vegetarian Option:** If you prefer a vegetarian version, skip the ham and use smoked paprika or a bit of liquid smoke to add a smoky flavor. You can also add a touch of soy sauce for depth.
- **Texture:** The soup will thicken as it sits. If it becomes too thick, you can add more broth or water to reach your desired consistency.
- **Storage:** Split pea soup keeps well in the refrigerator for up to 5 days and can be frozen for up to 3 months. Reheat thoroughly before serving.

This split pea soup is nourishing and comforting, with a great balance of flavors and textures. Enjoy it on a chilly day or as a filling lunch!

Maple Bacon Doughnuts

Ingredients:

For the Doughnuts:

- 2 1/4 teaspoons active dry yeast (1 packet)
- 1/4 cup warm milk (110°F/43°C)
- 1/4 cup granulated sugar
- 1/2 teaspoon salt
- 2 large eggs
- 1/4 cup unsalted butter, softened
- 2 1/2 cups all-purpose flour
- Vegetable oil (for frying)

For the Maple Glaze:

- 1 1/2 cups powdered sugar
- 1/4 cup pure maple syrup
- 2 tablespoons milk
- 1/2 teaspoon vanilla extract

For the Bacon Topping:

- 6 strips of bacon, cooked until crispy and crumbled

Instructions:

1. **Prepare the Dough:**
     - In a small bowl, dissolve the yeast in the warm milk with a pinch of sugar. Let it sit for about 5 minutes, or until it becomes frothy.
     - In a large bowl, combine the remaining sugar, salt, eggs, and softened butter. Mix well.
     - Add the yeast mixture and stir until combined.
     - Gradually add the flour, mixing until a soft dough forms.
     - Turn the dough out onto a lightly floured surface and knead for about 5-7 minutes, until smooth and elastic.
     - Place the dough in a lightly greased bowl, cover with a clean kitchen towel, and let it rise in a warm place for about 1-1.5 hours, or until doubled in size.
2. **Shape the Doughnuts:**
     - Punch down the risen dough and turn it out onto a lightly floured surface.
     - Roll out the dough to about 1/2 inch thickness.

- Use a doughnut cutter or two round cookie cutters (one large and one small for the hole) to cut out doughnuts.
- Place the cut doughnuts on a parchment-lined baking sheet, cover, and let them rise for another 30 minutes.

3. **Fry the Doughnuts:**
   - Heat about 2 inches of vegetable oil in a large, deep skillet or Dutch oven to 350°F (175°C).
   - Fry the doughnuts in batches, being careful not to overcrowd the pan. Fry for about 1-2 minutes per side, or until golden brown.
   - Remove the doughnuts with a slotted spoon and drain them on paper towels.
4. **Prepare the Maple Glaze:**
   - In a medium bowl, whisk together the powdered sugar, maple syrup, milk, and vanilla extract until smooth and slightly runny.
5. **Glaze and Top the Doughnuts:**
   - Dip the warm doughnuts into the maple glaze, allowing any excess to drip off.
   - Place the glazed doughnuts on a wire rack to set.
   - Immediately sprinkle the crumbled bacon on top of the glazed doughnuts before the glaze sets.
6. **Serve:**
   - Enjoy the doughnuts fresh and warm, with the crispy bacon adding a savory crunch to the sweet maple glaze.

Tips:

- **Oil Temperature:** Keep the oil temperature consistent for even frying. Too hot and the doughnuts will brown too quickly on the outside without cooking through; too cool and they will absorb too much oil.
- **Bacon:** For an extra crispy bacon topping, bake the bacon in the oven on a rack to allow the fat to drain away.
- **Glaze:** If the glaze is too thick, add a little more milk. If it's too thin, add more powdered sugar.

These Maple Bacon Doughnuts are a perfect blend of sweet and savory, making them a delightful treat for any occasion. Enjoy!

Cedar-Plank Salmon

Ingredients:

- **For the Cedar Plank:**
    - 1 cedar plank (about 12x6 inches or 30x15 cm), untreated and preferably pre-soaked
- **For the Salmon:**
    - 4 salmon fillets (about 6 oz or 170g each)
    - 2 tablespoons olive oil
    - 2 tablespoons brown sugar
    - 2 tablespoons soy sauce
    - 1 tablespoon Dijon mustard
    - 2 cloves garlic, minced
    - 1 tablespoon fresh lemon juice
    - 1 teaspoon dried thyme (or 1 tablespoon fresh thyme, chopped)
    - Salt and black pepper to taste
- **For Garnish (optional):**
    - Fresh dill or parsley, chopped
    - Lemon wedges

Instructions:

1. **Prepare the Cedar Plank:**
    1. Soak the cedar plank in water for at least 1-2 hours before cooking. This helps prevent it from catching fire on the grill. For best results, soak it overnight.
    2. After soaking, drain and pat the plank dry. You can also soak it in a mixture of water and white wine or beer for added flavor.
2. **Prepare the Salmon:**
    1. In a small bowl, mix together the olive oil, brown sugar, soy sauce, Dijon mustard, minced garlic, lemon juice, and thyme.
    2. Season the salmon fillets with salt and black pepper on both sides.
    3. Brush the salmon fillets with the marinade mixture, making sure they are well coated. Let them marinate for about 15-30 minutes.
3. **Grill or Bake the Salmon:**
   Grilling:
    1. Preheat your grill to medium heat (about 350°F or 175°C).
    2. Place the soaked cedar plank on the grill grates and close the lid. Heat it for about 5 minutes until it starts to smoke and crackle.
    3. Place the marinated salmon fillets on the cedar plank, skin side down. Close the lid and grill for 15-20 minutes, or until the salmon is cooked through and flakes easily with a fork. The exact time will depend on the thickness of the fillets.

4. If the plank starts to burn excessively, move it to a cooler part of the grill or reduce the heat.

4. **Baking:**
   1. Preheat your oven to 375°F (190°C).
   2. Place the soaked cedar plank on a baking sheet.
   3. Place the marinated salmon fillets on the cedar plank, skin side down.
   4. Bake in the preheated oven for 20-25 minutes, or until the salmon is cooked through and flakes easily with a fork.
5. **Serve:**
   1. Carefully transfer the cedar plank with the salmon to a serving platter.
   2. Garnish with fresh dill or parsley and serve with lemon wedges.

Tips:

- **Plank Safety:** Ensure your cedar plank is untreated and free of any chemicals or additives. Avoid using planks that have been pre-treated with oils or other substances.
- **Marinade Variations:** Feel free to adjust the marinade ingredients to your taste, adding things like honey, ginger, or additional herbs.
- **Salmon Doneness:** The internal temperature of cooked salmon should be 145°F (63°C). If you have a meat thermometer, use it to ensure perfect doneness.

Cedar-Plank Salmon is not only flavorful but also makes for a stunning presentation. The smoky aroma from the cedar plank elevates the salmon, making it a delicious and memorable dish. Enjoy!

Cornish Pasties

Ingredients:

For the Pastry:

- 2 1/2 cups (315g) all-purpose flour
- 1 teaspoon salt
- 1/2 cup (115g) unsalted butter, cold and diced
- 1/4 cup (50g) vegetable shortening (optional for extra flakiness)
- 1 large egg
- 4-6 tablespoons cold water

For the Filling:

- 1/2 pound (225g) beef skirt or chuck, finely chopped or ground
- 1 medium potato, peeled and finely diced
- 1 medium onion, finely diced
- 1 medium swede (rutabaga), peeled and finely diced
- 1 tablespoon fresh parsley, chopped (optional)
- 1 teaspoon salt
- 1/2 teaspoon black pepper
- 1/2 teaspoon dried thyme (optional)
- 1 tablespoon Worcestershire sauce (optional)

For Assembly:

- 1 egg, beaten (for egg wash)

Instructions:

1. **Prepare the Pastry:**
    1. In a large bowl, mix the flour and salt.
    2. Cut in the cold butter and vegetable shortening (if using) using a pastry cutter or your fingers until the mixture resembles coarse crumbs.
    3. In a small bowl, whisk the egg and add 4 tablespoons of cold water.
    4. Gradually add the egg mixture to the flour mixture, stirring until the dough starts to come together. Add more water, one tablespoon at a time, if needed.
    5. Turn the dough out onto a lightly floured surface and knead briefly until smooth.
    6. Divide the dough into 4-6 equal portions, shape into discs, wrap in plastic wrap, and refrigerate for at least 30 minutes.
2. **Prepare the Filling:**

1. In a large bowl, combine the chopped beef, diced potato, diced onion, and diced swede.
2. Season with salt, black pepper, thyme (if using), parsley (if using), and Worcestershire sauce (if using). Mix well to combine.

3. **Assemble the Pasties:**
    1. Preheat your oven to 375°F (190°C).
    2. On a lightly floured surface, roll out each dough disc into a circle about 1/8 inch (3mm) thick.
    3. Spoon a generous portion of the filling onto one half of each pastry circle, leaving a border around the edge.
    4. Fold the pastry over the filling to create a half-moon shape. Press the edges together to seal. You can crimp the edges with a fork or make a decorative crimp by pinching the edges together.
    5. Place the assembled pasties on a baking sheet lined with parchment paper.
    6. Brush the tops with the beaten egg to give them a golden finish.

4. **Bake:**
    1. Bake the pasties in the preheated oven for 45-55 minutes, or until the pastry is golden brown and the filling is cooked through.
    2. Allow the pasties to cool slightly before serving.

Tips:

- **Filling Variations:** You can add other vegetables like carrots or parsnips, or use different cuts of beef if preferred.
- **Make-Ahead:** Pasties can be assembled ahead of time and frozen. Bake from frozen, adding extra time as needed.
- **Serving:** Pasties are great served warm or at room temperature. They're perfect for lunch, a picnic, or a hearty snack.

Cornish pasties are hearty and satisfying, with a deliciously flaky crust and savory filling. Enjoy making and eating these traditional British pastries!

Wild Blueberry Pie

Ingredients:

For the Pie Crust:

- 2 1/2 cups all-purpose flour
- 1 teaspoon salt
- 1 tablespoon granulated sugar
- 1 cup (230g) unsalted butter, cold and cut into small cubes
- 6-8 tablespoons ice water

For the Filling:

- 4 cups wild blueberries (fresh or frozen; if using frozen, do not thaw)
- 3/4 cup granulated sugar
- 1/4 cup cornstarch
- 1/4 teaspoon salt
- 1 tablespoon lemon juice
- 1 teaspoon lemon zest
- 1/2 teaspoon vanilla extract
- 1/4 teaspoon ground cinnamon (optional)
- 1/4 teaspoon ground nutmeg (optional)

For Assembly:

- 1 egg, beaten (for egg wash)
- 1 tablespoon granulated sugar (for sprinkling)

Instructions:

1. **Prepare the Pie Crust:**
    1. In a large bowl, whisk together the flour, salt, and sugar.
    2. Add the cold butter cubes and cut into the flour mixture using a pastry cutter, fork, or your fingers until the mixture resembles coarse crumbs.
    3. Gradually add ice water, one tablespoon at a time, until the dough just comes together. Avoid overmixing.
    4. Divide the dough into two equal portions, shape each into a disc, wrap in plastic wrap, and refrigerate for at least 1 hour.
2. **Prepare the Filling:**
    1. In a large bowl, gently toss the wild blueberries with sugar, cornstarch, salt, lemon juice, lemon zest, vanilla extract, cinnamon, and nutmeg (if using).

2. Let the mixture sit for about 15 minutes to allow the flavors to meld and the cornstarch to absorb the juices.
3. **Assemble the Pie:**
   1. Preheat your oven to 375°F (190°C).
   2. On a lightly floured surface, roll out one disc of dough to fit your pie dish (about 12 inches in diameter). Transfer it to a 9-inch pie dish and trim the edges, leaving a slight overhang.
   3. Spoon the blueberry filling into the crust.
   4. Roll out the second disc of dough and place it over the filling. You can either cover the pie with a full crust or cut the dough into strips and create a lattice pattern.
   5. Trim and crimp the edges of the pie crust to seal.
   6. Brush the top crust with the beaten egg and sprinkle with granulated sugar for a golden finish.
4. **Bake:**
   1. Place the pie on a baking sheet (to catch any drips) and bake in the preheated oven for 45-55 minutes, or until the crust is golden brown and the filling is bubbly.
   2. If the crust starts to brown too quickly, you can cover the edges with foil to prevent burning.
   3. Allow the pie to cool for at least 2 hours before serving. This allows the filling to set and makes slicing easier.

Tips:

- **Frozen Blueberries:** If using frozen blueberries, do not thaw them before adding to the filling. This helps prevent the filling from becoming too watery.
- **Crust:** For a flakier crust, make sure your butter is very cold and avoid overworking the dough.
- **Thickening:** If you prefer a thicker filling, you can increase the amount of cornstarch slightly or use a mixture of cornstarch and flour.

Wild blueberry pie is a classic dessert that's perfect for summer or any time you want to enjoy the vibrant flavors of wild blueberries. Enjoy your homemade pie with a scoop of vanilla ice cream or a dollop of whipped cream for an extra treat!

Nova Scotia Lobster Roll

Ingredients:

For the Lobster Filling:

- 1 1/2 pounds (680g) cooked lobster meat (about 2 cups), chopped into bite-sized pieces
- 1/4 cup mayonnaise
- 1 tablespoon fresh lemon juice
- 1 tablespoon chopped fresh parsley
- 1 tablespoon finely chopped celery
- 1 tablespoon finely chopped red onion
- Salt and freshly ground black pepper to taste
- 1 teaspoon Dijon mustard (optional)
- 1 teaspoon Old Bay seasoning (optional)

For the Rolls:

- 4 hot dog buns or split-top rolls
- 2 tablespoons unsalted butter, melted
- Fresh lettuce leaves (optional, for garnish)
- Lemon wedges (for serving)

Instructions:

1. **Prepare the Lobster Filling:**
    1. In a large bowl, combine the chopped lobster meat, mayonnaise, lemon juice, chopped parsley, celery, and red onion.
    2. Season with salt and black pepper to taste. Add Dijon mustard and Old Bay seasoning if using. Mix gently until well combined.
    3. Cover and refrigerate the lobster mixture while you prepare the rolls.
2. **Prepare the Rolls:**
    1. Preheat a skillet or griddle over medium heat.
    2. Brush the cut sides of the buns with melted butter.
    3. Place the buns, cut side down, on the skillet and toast until golden brown and crisp, about 2-3 minutes.
3. **Assemble the Lobster Rolls:**
    1. If using lettuce, place a leaf in each toasted bun.
    2. Spoon the lobster filling evenly into each bun.
    3. Garnish with additional parsley if desired.
4. **Serve:**
    1. Serve the lobster rolls immediately, with lemon wedges on the side for an extra burst of freshness.

Tips:

- **Lobster Meat:** For the best flavor, use fresh lobster meat. You can also use pre-cooked lobster meat from the seafood counter or frozen lobster meat if fresh is not available. Make sure to thaw frozen lobster meat and drain well before using.
- **Mayonnaise:** Adjust the amount of mayonnaise to your preference for creaminess. You can also use a combination of mayonnaise and sour cream or Greek yogurt for a slightly different flavor and texture.
- **Toasting Rolls:** To ensure the rolls don't get soggy, toast them just before serving.

The Nova Scotia Lobster Roll is all about letting the fresh lobster shine. It's simple yet luxurious, perfect for a special occasion or a treat on a summer day. Enjoy!

Saskatoon Berry Jam

Ingredients:

- 4 cups Saskatoon berries (fresh or frozen)
- 1/4 cup lemon juice (about 2 lemons)
- 1 package (1.75 oz or 49g) fruit pectin (such as Sure-Jell)
- 5 cups granulated sugar
- 1/2 teaspoon butter (optional, to reduce foaming)

Instructions:

1. **Prepare the Berries:**
    1. If using fresh Saskatoon berries, rinse them thoroughly and remove any stems or leaves. If using frozen berries, thaw them and drain any excess liquid.
2. **Prepare Jars and Lids:**
    1. Sterilize your canning jars and lids by placing them in a boiling water bath for 10 minutes or running them through the dishwasher on a hot cycle. Keep them hot until you're ready to fill them.
3. **Cook the Jam:**
    1. In a large pot, combine the Saskatoon berries and lemon juice. Mash the berries slightly using a potato masher or the back of a spoon.
    2. Stir in the fruit pectin and bring the mixture to a boil over medium-high heat, stirring constantly.
    3. Once boiling, add the granulated sugar all at once, stirring continuously.
    4. Bring the mixture back to a full rolling boil (one that cannot be stirred down) and boil for exactly 1 minute, continuing to stir.
    5. Remove the pot from the heat. If you see foam on top, you can stir in a small amount of butter to reduce it.
4. **Test the Jam:**
    1. To test the jam's consistency, place a small spoonful of the hot jam onto a cold plate and let it sit for 1 minute. Run your finger through the jam; if it wrinkles and holds its shape, it's ready to be jarred. If not, return to a boil for an additional minute and test again.
5. **Fill the Jars:**
    1. Using a ladle and a canning funnel, pour the hot jam into the prepared jars, leaving about 1/4 inch (6mm) of headspace.
    2. Wipe the rims of the jars with a clean, damp cloth to remove any residue.
    3. Place the sterilized lids on the jars and screw on the metal bands until fingertip-tight.
6. **Process the Jars:**

1. Process the jars in a boiling water bath for 5-10 minutes to ensure they are sealed properly. The water should cover the jars by at least 1 inch (2.5 cm).
2. Remove the jars from the water bath and let them cool on a clean towel or rack for 24 hours.

7. **Check the Seals:**
   1. After cooling, check the seals by pressing down in the center of each lid. If it doesn't pop back, the jar is sealed. If any jars did not seal properly, refrigerate them and use within a few weeks.
8. **Store:**
   1. Store the sealed jars in a cool, dark place. Properly processed and sealed jars of Saskatoon berry jam can be stored for up to a year.

Tips:

- **Fruit Pectin:** Be sure to use fruit pectin specifically designed for making jams and jellies for the best results.
- **Headspace:** Leaving proper headspace in the jars helps ensure a good seal and prevents overflow during processing.
- **Consistency:** If you prefer a thicker jam, you can increase the cooking time slightly, but be cautious not to overcook as it can lead to a jam that is too stiff.

Saskatoon berry jam has a wonderful, unique flavor that makes it a delightful addition to your breakfast or as a gift. Enjoy making and savoring this special treat!

Maple Syrup Pie

Ingredients:

For the Pie Crust:

- 1 1/2 cups (190g) all-purpose flour
- 1/2 teaspoon salt
- 1/2 cup (115g) unsalted butter, cold and cut into small cubes
- 1/4 cup (50g) granulated sugar
- 1 large egg yolk
- 2-4 tablespoons ice water

For the Maple Syrup Filling:

- 1 cup (240ml) pure maple syrup
- 1/2 cup (120ml) heavy cream
- 1/4 cup (50g) packed brown sugar
- 2 large eggs
- 2 tablespoons unsalted butter, melted
- 1 teaspoon vanilla extract
- 1/4 teaspoon salt

Instructions:

1. **Prepare the Pie Crust:**
    1. In a large bowl, combine the flour and salt.
    2. Cut in the cold butter using a pastry cutter, fork, or your fingers until the mixture resembles coarse crumbs.
    3. Stir in the granulated sugar.
    4. In a small bowl, whisk the egg yolk and add 2 tablespoons of ice water. Gradually add the egg mixture to the flour mixture, stirring until the dough just comes together. Add more ice water, one tablespoon at a time, if needed.
    5. Form the dough into a disk, wrap it in plastic wrap, and refrigerate for at least 1 hour.
2. **Prepare the Filling:**
    1. Preheat your oven to 375°F (190°C).
    2. In a medium saucepan, combine the maple syrup, heavy cream, and brown sugar. Heat over medium heat, stirring until the sugar is dissolved. Remove from heat and let cool slightly.
    3. In a large bowl, whisk together the eggs, melted butter, vanilla extract, and salt.
    4. Gradually add the slightly cooled maple syrup mixture to the egg mixture, whisking constantly until well combined.

3. **Assemble the Pie:**
    1. On a lightly floured surface, roll out the chilled dough to fit a 9-inch (23 cm) pie dish. Transfer the dough to the pie dish, trim the excess, and crimp the edges.
    2. Pour the maple syrup filling into the prepared pie crust.
4. **Bake:**
    1. Place the pie on a baking sheet (to catch any drips) and bake in the preheated oven for 45-50 minutes, or until the filling is set and the top is golden brown. The filling should be slightly jiggly in the center when you remove it from the oven but will firm up as it cools.
    2. If the crust edges start to brown too quickly, cover them with aluminum foil to prevent burning.
5. **Cool and Serve:**
    1. Allow the pie to cool completely on a wire rack before slicing. This will help the filling set properly.
    2. Serve at room temperature or chilled. You can also top it with a dollop of whipped cream or a scoop of vanilla ice cream if desired.

Tips:

- **Maple Syrup:** Use pure maple syrup for the best flavor. Avoid imitation maple syrup, which is typically made from high fructose corn syrup.
- **Crust:** To avoid a soggy bottom, you can pre-bake the pie crust (blind bake) for about 10 minutes before adding the filling. Just make sure to let it cool slightly before filling it.
- **Filling Consistency:** If the filling seems too runny, bake it a little longer. The filling should be just set in the center when done.

Maple syrup pie is a deliciously sweet and comforting dessert that's perfect for showcasing the rich flavor of maple syrup. Enjoy making and savoring this delightful treat!

Crispy Samosas

Ingredients:

For the Pastry:

- 2 cups all-purpose flour
- 1/2 teaspoon salt
- 1/2 teaspoon caraway seeds (optional)
- 1/4 cup (60g) ghee or unsalted butter, melted
- 1/4 to 1/2 cup cold water

For the Filling:

- 2 tablespoons vegetable oil
- 1 teaspoon cumin seeds
- 1 teaspoon mustard seeds
- 1 medium onion, finely chopped
- 2 cloves garlic, minced
- 1 tablespoon fresh ginger, minced
- 2 medium potatoes, peeled and diced
- 1 cup frozen peas
- 1 medium carrot, peeled and finely diced
- 1 teaspoon ground coriander
- 1 teaspoon ground cumin
- 1/2 teaspoon turmeric powder
- 1/2 teaspoon garam masala
- 1/2 teaspoon chili powder (adjust to taste)
- Salt to taste
- 2 tablespoons fresh cilantro, chopped
- 1 tablespoon lemon juice

For Frying:

- Vegetable oil (for deep frying)

Instructions:

1. **Prepare the Pastry:**
    1. In a large bowl, combine the flour, salt, and caraway seeds (if using).
    2. Add the melted ghee or butter and mix until the mixture resembles coarse crumbs.

3. Gradually add cold water, a little at a time, until a smooth dough forms. The dough should be soft but not sticky.
   4. Cover the dough with a damp cloth or plastic wrap and let it rest for about 30 minutes.
2. **Prepare the Filling:**
   1. Heat the vegetable oil in a large pan over medium heat.
   2. Add the cumin seeds and mustard seeds. Cook for about 30 seconds until they start to pop.
   3. Add the chopped onion and cook until translucent and slightly golden.
   4. Stir in the garlic and ginger, and cook for another minute.
   5. Add the diced potatoes, peas, and carrots. Cook for about 5 minutes.
   6. Add the ground coriander, ground cumin, turmeric, garam masala, chili powder, and salt. Mix well and cook for another 5-7 minutes, or until the vegetables are tender.
   7. Stir in the fresh cilantro and lemon juice. Adjust seasoning if needed. Let the filling cool to room temperature.
3. **Assemble the Samosas:**
   1. Divide the rested dough into 12-16 equal portions and roll each portion into a thin circle about 6 inches (15 cm) in diameter.
   2. Cut each circle in half to form two semi-circles.
   3. Fold each semi-circle into a cone shape, sealing the edge with a little water.
   4. Fill the cone with a spoonful of the prepared filling, then seal the open edge by pinching the sides together to form a triangular shape. Ensure the edges are well sealed to prevent the filling from leaking out during frying.
   5. Repeat with the remaining dough and filling.
4. **Fry the Samosas:**
   1. Heat vegetable oil in a deep pan or fryer to 350°F (175°C).
   2. Carefully slide a few samosas into the hot oil, avoiding overcrowding the pan. Fry them in batches if necessary.
   3. Fry the samosas for about 4-5 minutes, or until they are golden brown and crispy, turning them occasionally for even cooking.
   4. Use a slotted spoon to remove the samosas from the oil and drain them on paper towels.
5. **Serve:**
   1. Serve the crispy samosas hot with chutney, yogurt sauce, or your favorite dipping sauce.

Tips:

- **Pastry Dough:** If the dough feels too dry, add a little more water. If it's too sticky, add a bit more flour.
- **Sealing:** Make sure the edges of the samosas are sealed well to prevent filling from leaking out during frying.

- **Baking Option:** For a healthier alternative, you can bake the samosas. Preheat your oven to 400°F (200°C), brush the samosas with oil, and bake for 20-25 minutes or until golden and crispy.

Crispy samosas are a versatile and delicious treat that can be enjoyed as a snack or appetizer. Enjoy making and eating these flavorful pockets of goodness!

Caribou Stew

Ingredients:

- 2 pounds (900g) caribou meat (or substitute with beef), cut into 1-inch cubes
- 2 tablespoons vegetable oil
- 1 large onion, chopped
- 3 cloves garlic, minced
- 3 carrots, peeled and sliced
- 3 potatoes, peeled and cubed
- 2 parsnips, peeled and sliced (optional)
- 1 cup celery, chopped
- 1 cup turnip, peeled and cubed (optional)
- 2 tablespoons tomato paste
- 4 cups beef or vegetable broth
- 1 cup red wine (optional, for richer flavor)
- 2 bay leaves
- 1 teaspoon dried thyme
- 1 teaspoon dried rosemary
- Salt and freshly ground black pepper to taste
- 1 cup frozen peas
- 2 tablespoons all-purpose flour (optional, for thickening)
- 2 tablespoons water (if using flour)

Instructions:

1. **Prepare the Meat:**
    1. Heat the vegetable oil in a large pot or Dutch oven over medium-high heat.
    2. Add the caribou meat cubes in batches (to avoid overcrowding) and brown them on all sides. Remove the meat from the pot and set it aside.
2. **Sauté the Vegetables:**
    1. In the same pot, add the chopped onion and cook until softened and translucent, about 5 minutes.
    2. Add the minced garlic and cook for an additional 1 minute.
3. **Build the Stew:**
    1. Stir in the tomato paste and cook for 2 minutes.
    2. Return the browned caribou meat to the pot.
    3. Add the carrots, potatoes, parsnips, celery, and turnip (if using).
    4. Pour in the beef or vegetable broth and red wine (if using).
    5. Add the bay leaves, dried thyme, dried rosemary, salt, and black pepper. Stir well.
4. **Simmer the Stew:**

1. Bring the mixture to a boil.
2. Reduce the heat to low, cover, and let it simmer for about 1.5 to 2 hours, or until the meat and vegetables are tender. Stir occasionally.
3. If you prefer a thicker stew, mix the flour with water to form a slurry, and stir it into the stew during the last 30 minutes of cooking. This will help thicken the broth.

5. **Add Peas:**
   1. About 10 minutes before serving, stir in the frozen peas.
6. **Adjust Seasoning:**
   1. Taste the stew and adjust seasoning with additional salt and pepper if needed.
7. **Serve:**
   1. Serve the caribou stew hot with crusty bread or over a bed of rice or mashed potatoes.

Tips:

- **Meat Tenderness:** Caribou meat can be lean, so cooking it slowly helps ensure it stays tender. If using beef, choose cuts like chuck or stew meat for similar results.
- **Vegetables:** Feel free to adjust the vegetable selection based on what you have on hand or your preferences.
- **Wine:** Red wine adds depth to the stew, but you can omit it if preferred or substitute with additional broth.

Caribou stew is a comforting and hearty dish perfect for cold days, providing a rich and satisfying meal that celebrates the unique flavor of caribou meat. Enjoy!

Ketchup Chips

Ingredients:

For the Potato Chips:

- 4 large russet potatoes
- 1 tablespoon white vinegar
- 2 tablespoons vegetable oil
- Salt (to taste)

For the Ketchup Seasoning:

- 1 tablespoon tomato powder (or ketchup powder)
- 1 tablespoon granulated sugar
- 1 teaspoon onion powder
- 1 teaspoon garlic powder
- 1/2 teaspoon paprika
- 1/4 teaspoon cayenne pepper (optional, for heat)
- 1/4 teaspoon salt
- 1/4 teaspoon dried oregano (optional)
- 1/4 teaspoon dried thyme (optional)

Instructions:

1. **Prepare the Potatoes:**
    1. Peel the potatoes and slice them thinly (about 1/16 inch or 1.5 mm thick) using a mandoline or a sharp knife.
    2. Place the potato slices in a large bowl of cold water with 1 tablespoon of white vinegar. Let them soak for at least 30 minutes to remove excess starch and help them crisp up during frying.
2. **Preheat Oil:**
    1. Heat vegetable oil in a deep fryer or a large heavy-bottomed pot to 350°F (175°C). Use enough oil to submerge the potato slices.
3. **Dry the Potatoes:**
    1. Drain the potato slices and pat them thoroughly dry with paper towels. It's important to remove as much moisture as possible to avoid splattering and ensure crispiness.
4. **Fry the Chips:**
    1. Carefully add a small batch of potato slices to the hot oil, making sure not to overcrowd the pot.
    2. Fry the slices for 2-4 minutes, or until golden brown and crispy. Stir occasionally to ensure even cooking.

3. Use a slotted spoon to remove the chips from the oil and drain them on paper towels. Sprinkle with a little salt while still hot.
4. Repeat with the remaining potato slices.

5. **Prepare the Ketchup Seasoning:**
   1. In a small bowl, mix together the tomato powder, granulated sugar, onion powder, garlic powder, paprika, cayenne pepper (if using), salt, dried oregano, and dried thyme.

6. **Season the Chips:**
   1. While the chips are still warm, toss them in a large bowl with the ketchup seasoning mix until evenly coated. You can also use a large resealable bag to shake the chips with the seasoning for an even coating.

7. **Cool and Store:**
   1. Let the seasoned chips cool completely on a wire rack. They will become crispier as they cool.
   2. Store the chips in an airtight container to keep them fresh and crispy.

Tips:

- **Potato Slices:** Thin slices will result in crispier chips, while thicker slices will be more on the crunchy side.
- **Oil Temperature:** Ensure the oil is at the correct temperature to prevent the chips from becoming greasy. Use a candy thermometer to monitor the temperature.
- **Ketchup Powder:** If you can't find ketchup powder, you can use a small amount of ketchup paste mixed with the dry seasonings, but it may not coat the chips as evenly.

Homemade ketchup chips are a fun and tasty snack that capture the beloved flavor of the classic Canadian treat. Enjoy your crispy, tangy chips!

Yellow Pea Soup

Ingredients:

- 1 pound (450g) dried yellow split peas
- 2 tablespoons vegetable oil
- 1 large onion, chopped
- 2 cloves garlic, minced
- 3 large carrots, peeled and chopped
- 3 celery stalks, chopped
- 1 large potato, peeled and diced
- 1 bay leaf
- 1 teaspoon dried thyme
- 1 teaspoon dried rosemary (optional)
- 8 cups (2 liters) vegetable or chicken broth
- 1-2 smoked ham hocks or 1 cup diced ham (optional, for added flavor)
- Salt and freshly ground black pepper to taste
- 2 tablespoons fresh parsley, chopped (for garnish)
- 1 tablespoon lemon juice (optional, for brightness)

Instructions:

1. **Prepare the Peas:**
    1. Rinse the dried yellow split peas under cold running water. Pick out any debris or damaged peas. No need to soak the peas, but you can if you prefer.
2. **Sauté Vegetables:**
    1. Heat the vegetable oil in a large pot or Dutch oven over medium heat.
    2. Add the chopped onion and cook until softened and translucent, about 5 minutes.
    3. Stir in the minced garlic and cook for another minute.
3. **Add Vegetables and Spices:**
    1. Add the chopped carrots, celery, and potato to the pot. Cook for about 5 minutes, stirring occasionally.
    2. Add the bay leaf, dried thyme, and dried rosemary (if using). Stir well.
4. **Cook the Soup:**
    1. Add the rinsed yellow split peas and the broth to the pot. Stir to combine.
    2. If using, add the smoked ham hocks or diced ham. Bring the mixture to a boil.
    3. Reduce the heat to low, cover, and let it simmer for about 1 to 1.5 hours, or until the peas are tender and the soup has thickened. Stir occasionally, and add more broth or water if the soup becomes too thick.
5. **Blend the Soup (Optional):**
    1. For a smoother texture, you can blend the soup with an immersion blender directly in the pot until it reaches your desired consistency. Alternatively, you can

transfer batches of the soup to a countertop blender. Be careful when blending hot liquids.

6. **Season and Adjust:**
   1. Remove the bay leaf and any ham hocks from the soup. If using ham hocks, shred any meat from the bones and return it to the soup.
   2. Season the soup with salt and freshly ground black pepper to taste.
   3. Stir in the lemon juice if using, which adds a nice brightness to the soup.
7. **Serve:**
   1. Ladle the soup into bowls and garnish with fresh parsley.

Tips:

- **Consistency:** Yellow pea soup thickens as it sits, so you might need to add a bit more broth or water when reheating leftovers.
- **Ham:** If you're not using ham hocks or diced ham, you can add a smoked turkey leg or omit the meat for a vegetarian version. Adjust seasoning accordingly.
- **Vegetables:** Feel free to add other vegetables like leeks, parsnips, or bell peppers based on your preference.

Yellow pea soup is a comforting and nourishing meal that's perfect for cold weather or whenever you need a hearty, satisfying dish. Enjoy!

Liver and Onions

Ingredients:

- 1 pound (450g) beef or calf liver, sliced into 1/2-inch (1.3 cm) thick pieces
- 2 large onions, thinly sliced
- 1/2 cup all-purpose flour
- Salt and freshly ground black pepper to taste
- 2 tablespoons vegetable oil or butter
- 1/2 cup beef broth (optional, for added flavor)
- 1 tablespoon balsamic vinegar or red wine vinegar (optional, for a touch of acidity)
- Fresh parsley, chopped (for garnish)

Instructions:

1. **Prepare the Liver:**
    1. Rinse the liver slices under cold water and pat them dry with paper towels.
    2. Season the liver slices with salt and pepper.
    3. Dredge each slice in flour, shaking off any excess. This will help create a nice crust when cooked.
2. **Cook the Onions:**
    1. Heat 1 tablespoon of vegetable oil or butter in a large skillet over medium heat.
    2. Add the sliced onions and cook, stirring occasionally, until they are soft and caramelized, about 15-20 minutes. Remove the onions from the skillet and set them aside.
3. **Cook the Liver:**
    1. In the same skillet, add the remaining tablespoon of oil or butter over medium-high heat.
    2. Add the liver slices and cook for about 2-3 minutes per side, or until they are browned on the outside but still slightly pink in the center. Avoid overcooking, as liver can become tough if cooked too long.
    3. If using beef broth, pour it into the skillet and let it simmer for 2-3 minutes to deglaze the pan and create a bit of sauce. If using vinegar, add it in this step.
4. **Combine and Serve:**
    1. Return the caramelized onions to the skillet with the liver and let them heat through together, about 2 minutes.
    2. Taste and adjust seasoning with more salt and pepper if needed.
    3. Garnish with chopped fresh parsley if desired.
5. **Serve:**
    1. Serve the liver and onions hot, with mashed potatoes, rice, or a side of vegetables.

Tips:

- **Liver Preparation:** If the liver has a strong flavor that you find off-putting, you can soak it in milk for about an hour before cooking. This can help mellow the taste.
- **Onions:** For extra flavor, you can add a pinch of sugar to the onions as they caramelize to enhance their sweetness.
- **Sauce:** If you prefer a thicker sauce, you can make a slurry with 1 tablespoon of flour and 2 tablespoons of water and stir it into the pan with the broth.

Liver and onions is a traditional dish that's both flavorful and nutritious. With the right preparation, it can be a truly satisfying meal. Enjoy!

Canadian Bacon and Eggs

Ingredients:

- **For the Canadian Bacon:**
    - 4 slices of Canadian bacon (also known as back bacon)
    - 1 tablespoon vegetable oil or butter
- **For the Eggs:**
    - 4 large eggs
    - 1 tablespoon butter or oil (for cooking the eggs)
    - Salt and freshly ground black pepper to taste
    - Fresh chives or parsley, chopped (optional, for garnish)

Instructions:

1. **Cook the Canadian Bacon:**
    - Heat a large skillet over medium heat.
    - Add the vegetable oil or butter.
    - Once hot, add the Canadian bacon slices.
    - Cook the bacon for about 2-3 minutes on each side, or until it is browned and slightly crisped. Canadian bacon is pre-cooked, so you're mainly heating it through and adding some color.
    - Remove the bacon from the skillet and set it aside on a plate. Keep warm.
2. **Cook the Eggs:**
    - In the same skillet, add 1 tablespoon of butter or oil.
    - Heat until melted and hot.
    - Crack the eggs into the skillet. You can cook them to your preference:
        - **Sunny Side Up:** Cook for about 2-3 minutes without flipping until the whites are set but the yolks are still runny.
        - **Over Easy/Medium/Hard:** Cook for 2-3 minutes on the first side, then flip gently and cook for an additional 1-2 minutes for over-easy, 3-4 minutes for over-medium, or until the yolks are fully cooked for over-hard.
        - **Scrambled:** Beat the eggs in a bowl, pour them into the skillet, and cook, stirring frequently, until they are fully cooked and set.
    - Season with salt and freshly ground black pepper.
3. **Assemble and Serve:**
    - Place the cooked Canadian bacon slices on plates.
    - Top with the cooked eggs.
    - Garnish with fresh chives or parsley if desired.
4. **Accompaniments (Optional):**
    - Serve with toast, hash browns, fresh fruit, or a side of vegetables for a complete breakfast.

Tips:

- **Egg Cooking Tips:** If you're cooking eggs sunny side up, avoid overcrowding the skillet to ensure even cooking.
- **Canadian Bacon Alternatives:** If you don't have Canadian bacon, you can use regular bacon or ham. Adjust cooking times accordingly.

This breakfast is quick, versatile, and packed with protein, making it an excellent way to start your day. Enjoy your Canadian bacon and eggs!

Salmon Gravlax

Ingredients:

- **For the Gravlax:**
    - 1 whole side of salmon, skin on, about 2 pounds (900g)
    - 1/4 cup kosher salt
    - 1/4 cup granulated sugar
    - 1 tablespoon black peppercorns, coarsely crushed
    - 1 tablespoon crushed coriander seeds
    - 1 tablespoon dill seeds (optional, for extra flavor)
    - 1 bunch fresh dill, chopped (about 1/2 cup packed)
    - 2 tablespoons vodka or aquavit (optional, for added flavor)
- **For Serving:**
    - Thinly sliced rye bread or bagels
    - Cream cheese or sour cream
    - Capers
    - Red onions, thinly sliced
    - Lemon wedges
    - Additional fresh dill for garnish

Instructions:

1. **Prepare the Salmon:**
    1. Ensure the salmon is boneless and skinless, or remove any pin bones using tweezers.
    2. Rinse the salmon under cold water and pat dry with paper towels.
2. **Prepare the Cure Mixture:**
    1. In a bowl, mix together the kosher salt, granulated sugar, coarsely crushed black peppercorns, crushed coriander seeds, and dill seeds (if using).
3. **Apply the Cure:**
    1. Place a large piece of plastic wrap on a flat surface.
    2. Spread half of the cure mixture evenly over the surface of the plastic wrap.
    3. Place the salmon, skin side down, on top of the cure mixture.
    4. Sprinkle the remaining cure mixture evenly over the salmon, pressing it gently to adhere.
    5. Sprinkle the chopped fresh dill evenly over the salmon. If using vodka or aquavit, sprinkle it over the dill.
4. **Wrap and Refrigerate:**
    1. Carefully wrap the salmon tightly in the plastic wrap.
    2. Place the wrapped salmon on a plate or in a dish to catch any liquid that may drain out.

3. Place a heavy object (like a can or another plate) on top of the salmon to help press the cure mixture into the fish.
4. Refrigerate for 48 to 72 hours. Turn the salmon every 12-24 hours to ensure even curing.

5. **Prepare for Serving:**
    1. After the curing time, remove the salmon from the refrigerator and unwrap it.
    2. Rinse off the cure mixture under cold water and pat the salmon dry with paper towels.
    3. Slice the gravlax thinly at a slight angle, using a sharp knife.
6. **Serve:**
    1. Arrange the thinly sliced gravlax on a platter.
    2. Serve with thinly sliced rye bread or bagels, cream cheese or sour cream, capers, red onions, and lemon wedges.
    3. Garnish with additional fresh dill if desired.

Tips:

- **Salmon Quality:** Use high-quality, sushi-grade salmon for the best results since you're eating it raw.
- **Cure Mixture:** Adjust the amount of salt and sugar to your taste. If you prefer a less salty gravlax, you can reduce the amount of salt slightly.
- **Storage:** Gravlax can be stored in the refrigerator for up to a week. It also freezes well if you want to make it ahead of time.

Salmon gravlax is a versatile dish that's perfect for brunch, appetizers, or even as part of a festive spread. Enjoy making and serving this delightful treat!

Cedar Plank Grilled Trout

Ingredients:

- **For the Trout:**
    - 4 trout fillets (about 6-8 ounces each), skin on
    - 2 tablespoons olive oil
    - 2 cloves garlic, minced
    - 1 lemon, sliced
    - Fresh herbs (such as dill, thyme, or parsley), for garnish
    - Salt and freshly ground black pepper, to taste
- **For the Cedar Plank:**
    - 1 cedar plank (large enough to fit the trout fillets)
    - Water (for soaking)

Instructions:

1. **Prepare the Cedar Plank:**
    1. Soak the cedar plank in water for at least 1 hour before grilling. This helps prevent it from catching fire on the grill. For best results, soak it overnight if possible.
2. **Prepare the Trout:**
    1. Rinse the trout fillets under cold water and pat them dry with paper towels.
    2. Brush the fillets with olive oil and season them with salt and freshly ground black pepper.
    3. Rub the minced garlic over the fillets.
    4. Place a few lemon slices and fresh herbs on top of each fillet.
3. **Preheat the Grill:**
    1. Preheat your grill to medium heat (about 350°F to 375°F or 175°C to 190°C).
4. **Prepare the Cedar Plank:**
    1. Remove the cedar plank from the water and place it on the grill.
    2. Close the lid and let it heat up for about 5 minutes, or until you start to see smoke coming from the plank. This step helps to infuse the fish with a smoky flavor.
5. **Grill the Trout:**
    1. Place the seasoned trout fillets, skin side down, on the cedar plank.
    2. Close the lid of the grill and cook the trout for about 12-15 minutes, or until the fish is opaque and flakes easily with a fork. The cooking time can vary depending on the thickness of the fillets and the temperature of the grill.
    3. If the fish is done before the cedar plank has burned through, you can carefully transfer the fillets to a plate and cover them with foil to keep warm while the plank continues to smoke.
6. **Serve:**

1. Carefully remove the cedar plank from the grill and transfer the trout fillets to serving plates.
2. Garnish with additional fresh herbs and lemon wedges if desired.

Tips:

- **Cedar Plank:** Ensure that the cedar plank is untreated and free from any chemicals or additives. You can find cedar grilling planks at kitchen supply stores or online.
- **Fish Freshness:** Use fresh, high-quality trout for the best flavor and texture.
- **Grill Temperature:** Maintain a consistent medium heat to prevent the cedar plank from burning too quickly and to cook the trout evenly.

Cedar plank grilled trout is a simple yet elegant dish that brings out the natural flavors of the fish while adding a delicious smoky aroma. Enjoy this delightful and aromatic meal!

Roasted Root Vegetables

Ingredients:

- **Vegetables:**
    - 3 large carrots, peeled and cut into chunks
    - 2 large parsnips, peeled and cut into chunks
    - 1 large sweet potato, peeled and cut into chunks
    - 1 medium red or yellow beet, peeled and cut into chunks (optional)
    - 1 large onion, peeled and cut into wedges
    - 2-3 cloves garlic, peeled and left whole
    - 1 tablespoon fresh rosemary or thyme (or 1 teaspoon dried)
    - 2 tablespoons olive oil
    - Salt and freshly ground black pepper to taste

Instructions:

1. **Preheat Oven:**
    1. Preheat your oven to 425°F (220°C).
2. **Prepare the Vegetables:**
    1. Peel and cut all the vegetables into uniform chunks, roughly 1-inch (2.5 cm) pieces. This helps them cook evenly.
    2. Place the cut vegetables into a large bowl.
3. **Season the Vegetables:**
    1. Drizzle the olive oil over the vegetables.
    2. Add the fresh rosemary or thyme, salt, and pepper.
    3. Toss everything together until the vegetables are evenly coated with oil and seasonings.
4. **Roast the Vegetables:**
    1. Spread the vegetables out in a single layer on a baking sheet or roasting pan. For best results, use a pan with some space between the vegetables to ensure they roast rather than steam.
    2. Place the pan in the preheated oven.
    3. Roast for about 25-35 minutes, or until the vegetables are tender and caramelized. Stir or flip the vegetables halfway through roasting to ensure even cooking.
5. **Check for Doneness:**
    1. The vegetables are done when they are fork-tender and have a golden-brown, slightly crispy exterior.
6. **Serve:**
    1. Remove the vegetables from the oven and transfer them to a serving dish.
    2. Garnish with additional fresh herbs if desired.

Tips:

- **Variety:** Feel free to add other root vegetables like rutabaga, turnips, or potatoes for variety. Adjust cooking times if necessary.
- **Cut Size:** Ensure all the vegetables are cut to roughly the same size to ensure even cooking.
- **Seasoning:** Experiment with different herbs and spices to match your main dish. For example, paprika, garlic powder, or a pinch of cayenne can add extra flavor.

Roasted root vegetables are a versatile and easy-to-make side dish that adds warmth and depth to any meal. Enjoy their rich flavors and comforting texture!

Squash Soup

Ingredients:

- **For the Soup:**
    - 2 tablespoons olive oil or butter
    - 1 large onion, chopped
    - 2 cloves garlic, minced
    - 1 large butternut squash (about 3-4 pounds), peeled, seeded, and cubed
    - 1 large carrot, peeled and chopped
    - 1-2 stalks celery, chopped
    - 4 cups (1 liter) vegetable or chicken broth
    - 1 teaspoon ground cumin
    - 1/2 teaspoon ground nutmeg
    - 1/2 teaspoon ground ginger (optional)
    - Salt and freshly ground black pepper to taste
    - 1/2 cup heavy cream or coconut milk (optional, for creaminess)
    - 1 tablespoon maple syrup or honey (optional, for a touch of sweetness)
- **For Garnish:**
    - Fresh parsley or chives, chopped
    - A swirl of cream or coconut milk
    - Toasted pumpkin seeds or croutons

Instructions:

1. **Prepare the Squash:**
    1. Peel and seed the butternut squash. Cut it into 1-inch (2.5 cm) cubes. If using other squash types, prepare them similarly.
2. **Sauté Vegetables:**
    1. Heat the olive oil or butter in a large pot over medium heat.
    2. Add the chopped onion and cook until softened, about 5 minutes.
    3. Stir in the minced garlic and cook for another minute until fragrant.
3. **Add Squash and Broth:**
    1. Add the cubed butternut squash, chopped carrot, and celery to the pot.
    2. Pour in the vegetable or chicken broth.
    3. Stir in the ground cumin, ground nutmeg, and ground ginger (if using).
    4. Bring the mixture to a boil, then reduce the heat and let it simmer until the squash and other vegetables are tender, about 20-25 minutes.
4. **Blend the Soup:**
    1. Use an immersion blender to puree the soup directly in the pot until smooth. Alternatively, you can transfer the soup in batches to a countertop blender. Be cautious with hot liquids; blend in small batches if using a countertop blender.

2. If you prefer a chunky texture, you can blend just half of the soup and leave some chunks.
5. **Add Cream and Sweetener:**
   1. Stir in the heavy cream or coconut milk if using, and heat through.
   2. Add the maple syrup or honey if you like a touch of sweetness, and adjust the seasoning with salt and pepper to taste.
6. **Serve:**
   1. Ladle the soup into bowls.
   2. Garnish with fresh parsley or chives, a swirl of cream or coconut milk, and toasted pumpkin seeds or croutons if desired.

Tips:

- **Squash Variety:** Feel free to experiment with different types of squash, like acorn or kabocha, for different flavors and textures.
- **Spice Variations:** Customize the spices according to your taste. Add a pinch of cayenne for heat or curry powder for a different twist.
- **Cream Alternatives:** If you prefer a dairy-free version, use coconut milk or almond milk instead of heavy cream.

This squash soup is a versatile and comforting dish that can be enjoyed on its own or as a starter to a meal. Enjoy the rich, velvety texture and warm flavors!

Bison Burger

Ingredients:

- **For the Burgers:**
    - 1 pound (450g) ground bison
    - 1 tablespoon olive oil or melted butter
    - 1 teaspoon garlic powder
    - 1 teaspoon onion powder
    - 1 teaspoon smoked paprika
    - 1 teaspoon salt
    - 1/2 teaspoon freshly ground black pepper
    - 1 tablespoon Worcestershire sauce (optional, for added flavor)
    - 4 burger buns
    - Lettuce, tomato slices, onion slices, pickles, and cheese (optional, for toppings)
- **For Serving:**
    - Your favorite condiments (ketchup, mustard, mayo)
    - Additional toppings such as avocado, bacon, or sautéed mushrooms (optional)

Instructions:

1. **Prepare the Bison Patties:**
    1. In a large bowl, combine the ground bison with garlic powder, onion powder, smoked paprika, salt, black pepper, and Worcestershire sauce (if using). Mix gently until the seasonings are evenly distributed. Avoid overmixing, as it can make the burgers tough.
    2. Divide the mixture into 4 equal portions and shape each portion into a patty, about 3/4 inch (2 cm) thick. Press a small indentation in the center of each patty with your thumb. This helps the patties cook evenly and reduces puffing up in the center.
2. **Preheat the Grill or Pan:**
    1. Preheat your grill to medium-high heat (about 375°F to 400°F or 190°C to 200°C). If using a stovetop, heat a skillet or griddle over medium-high heat and add a little oil.
3. **Cook the Patties:**
    1. Place the bison patties on the grill or skillet.
    2. Cook the patties for about 4-5 minutes per side, or until they reach your desired level of doneness. Bison is best cooked medium-rare to medium, as it can become dry if overcooked. Use a meat thermometer to check the internal temperature (160°F or 70°C is recommended for ground meat).
    3. If adding cheese, place a slice on each patty during the last minute of cooking and cover to melt.

4. **Toast the Buns:**
    1. While the patties are cooking, split the burger buns and toast them on the grill or in a toaster until lightly golden.
5. **Assemble the Burgers:**
    1. Spread condiments on the bottom half of each toasted bun.
    2. Place the cooked bison patty on the bun.
    3. Add your desired toppings such as lettuce, tomato, onion, pickles, and cheese.
    4. Top with the other half of the bun.
6. **Serve:**
    1. Serve the bison burgers immediately with your favorite sides, such as fries, sweet potato fries, or a salad.

Tips:

- **Handling Bison:** Bison is leaner than beef, so handle it gently and avoid overworking the meat to keep the burgers tender.
- **Flavor Enhancements:** Feel free to experiment with different seasonings or marinades to suit your taste. Adding a bit of fresh herbs like rosemary or thyme can also enhance the flavor.
- **Resting:** Let the burgers rest for a few minutes after cooking to allow the juices to redistribute and keep them moist.

Bison burgers offer a lean, flavorful alternative to traditional beef burgers and can be customized with a variety of toppings and condiments to suit your preferences. Enjoy!

Sweet Corn Fritters

Ingredients:

- **For the Fritters:**
    - 1 cup fresh or frozen corn kernels (thawed if frozen)
    - 1 cup all-purpose flour
    - 1/2 cup cornmeal
    - 1 tablespoon sugar
    - 1 teaspoon baking powder
    - 1/2 teaspoon baking soda
    - 1/2 teaspoon salt
    - 1/4 teaspoon black pepper
    - 1/2 cup buttermilk (or milk with 1 tablespoon lemon juice or vinegar)
    - 1 large egg
    - 2 tablespoons finely chopped fresh chives or green onions (optional)
    - 1/4 cup grated cheese (optional, cheddar or Parmesan works well)
    - Vegetable oil for frying
- **For Serving (optional):**
    - Sour cream or Greek yogurt
    - Fresh herbs like parsley or cilantro
    - Hot sauce or ketchup

Instructions:

1. **Prepare the Ingredients:**
    1. If using fresh corn, cut the kernels off the cobs. If using frozen corn, thaw and drain it.
    2. In a large bowl, whisk together the flour, cornmeal, sugar, baking powder, baking soda, salt, and black pepper.
2. **Mix Wet Ingredients:**
    1. In a separate bowl, whisk together the buttermilk and egg until well combined.
    2. If using, stir in the chopped chives or green onions and grated cheese.
3. **Combine Ingredients:**
    1. Pour the wet ingredients into the dry ingredients and mix until just combined. The batter will be lumpy.
    2. Fold in the corn kernels until evenly distributed throughout the batter.
4. **Heat the Oil:**
    1. Heat about 1/4 inch (0.6 cm) of vegetable oil in a large skillet or frying pan over medium heat. You can test if the oil is ready by dropping a small amount of batter into the pan; it should sizzle and float to the top.
5. **Fry the Fritters:**

1. Spoon about 2 tablespoons of batter per fritter into the hot oil, flattening them slightly with the back of the spoon.
2. Fry the fritters for about 2-3 minutes on each side, or until they are golden brown and crispy.
3. Remove the fritters from the pan and place them on a paper towel-lined plate to drain any excess oil.

6. **Serve:**
    1. Serve the fritters warm, with optional toppings like sour cream, fresh herbs, or a drizzle of hot sauce.

Tips:

- **Corn:** Using fresh corn in season will give the fritters a sweet and juicy flavor. Frozen corn works well too, especially when fresh corn is not available.
- **Batter Consistency:** If the batter seems too thick, you can add a little more buttermilk to reach your desired consistency. It should be thick but spoonable.
- **Oil Temperature:** Make sure the oil is hot enough before adding the batter. If the oil is not hot enough, the fritters will absorb too much oil and become greasy.

Sweet corn fritters are versatile and can be enjoyed with various toppings and dipping sauces. They're perfect for a summer appetizer or a cozy side dish during cooler months. Enjoy!

Pork Tenderloin with Apples

Ingredients:

- **For the Pork Tenderloin:**
    - 1 to 1.5 pounds (450-680g) pork tenderloin
    - 2 tablespoons olive oil
    - 1 tablespoon Dijon mustard
    - 1 tablespoon brown sugar
    - 2 cloves garlic, minced
    - 1 teaspoon dried thyme or rosemary (or 1 tablespoon fresh thyme or rosemary)
    - Salt and freshly ground black pepper to taste
- **For the Apples:**
    - 2 large apples, peeled, cored, and sliced (such as Honeycrisp, Granny Smith, or Fuji)
    - 1 tablespoon butter
    - 2 tablespoons brown sugar
    - 1/2 teaspoon ground cinnamon
    - 1/4 teaspoon ground nutmeg (optional)
    - 1/4 cup apple cider or white wine
    - 1/4 cup chopped pecans or walnuts (optional, for added texture)
- **For Serving (optional):**
    - Fresh parsley or thyme for garnish
    - Extra apple slices or a sprinkle of additional cinnamon for garnish

Instructions:

1. **Prepare the Pork Tenderloin:**
    1. Preheat your oven to 400°F (200°C).
    2. Pat the pork tenderloin dry with paper towels and season it with salt and black pepper.
    3. In a small bowl, mix together the Dijon mustard, brown sugar, minced garlic, and dried thyme or rosemary.
    4. Rub this mixture all over the pork tenderloin.
2. **Sear the Pork:**
    1. Heat olive oil in an ovenproof skillet over medium-high heat.
    2. Once the oil is hot, add the pork tenderloin and sear it on all sides until browned, about 2-3 minutes per side.
3. **Prepare the Apples:**
    1. While the pork is searing, melt the butter in a separate skillet over medium heat.
    2. Add the apple slices and cook until they start to soften, about 3-4 minutes.
    3. Stir in the brown sugar, ground cinnamon, and nutmeg (if using).

4. Add the apple cider or white wine and cook until the apples are tender and the sauce has thickened slightly, about 5 minutes.
   5. Stir in the chopped pecans or walnuts if desired.
4. **Roast the Pork:**
   1. Once the pork is seared, transfer the skillet to the preheated oven.
   2. Roast the pork for about 15-20 minutes, or until the internal temperature reaches 145°F (63°C).
   3. Remove the pork from the oven and let it rest for 5 minutes before slicing.
5. **Combine and Serve:**
   1. Slice the pork tenderloin into medallions.
   2. Serve the sliced pork on a platter or individual plates, topped with the sautéed apples and their sauce.
   3. Garnish with fresh parsley or thyme and additional apple slices if desired.

Tips:

- **Resting the Pork:** Letting the pork rest after roasting helps keep it juicy and tender.
- **Apple Variety:** Choose apples that hold their shape well during cooking. Firm apples like Honeycrisp or Granny Smith work well.
- **Wine/Cider:** Apple cider adds a nice touch of sweetness, but you can use white wine or even a splash of water if preferred.

This pork tenderloin with apples is a comforting, flavorful dish that pairs wonderfully with sides like roasted vegetables, mashed potatoes, or a simple green salad. Enjoy!

Maple-Glazed Carrots

Ingredients:

- 1 pound (450g) baby carrots or regular carrots, peeled and cut into uniform pieces
- 2 tablespoons butter
- 1/4 cup pure maple syrup
- 2 tablespoons brown sugar
- 1/2 teaspoon ground cinnamon (optional)
- Salt and freshly ground black pepper to taste
- 1 tablespoon chopped fresh parsley or thyme for garnish (optional)

Instructions:

1. **Cook the Carrots:**
   1. **Boil or Steam:** If using whole baby carrots, you can cook them directly. If using regular carrots, peel and cut them into 1/2-inch (1.25 cm) thick slices.
   2. Place the carrots in a large pot and cover with water. Add a pinch of salt.
   3. Bring to a boil, then reduce the heat and simmer until the carrots are tender but still crisp, about 8-10 minutes. Alternatively, you can steam the carrots until tender.
   4. Drain the carrots and set aside.
2. **Prepare the Glaze:**
   1. In a large skillet, melt the butter over medium heat.
   2. Stir in the maple syrup, brown sugar, and ground cinnamon (if using).
   3. Cook, stirring frequently, until the sugar is dissolved and the mixture is smooth, about 2-3 minutes.
3. **Glaze the Carrots:**
   1. Add the cooked carrots to the skillet with the glaze.
   2. Toss the carrots in the glaze to coat them evenly.
   3. Continue cooking, stirring occasionally, until the carrots are heated through and the glaze has thickened slightly, about 5-7 minutes.
4. **Season and Serve:**
   1. Season the glazed carrots with salt and freshly ground black pepper to taste.
   2. Transfer the carrots to a serving dish and garnish with chopped fresh parsley or thyme if desired.

Tips:

- **Carrot Variety:** Baby carrots are convenient, but regular carrots offer more flavor. If using regular carrots, cut them into evenly sized pieces for uniform cooking.

- **Maple Syrup:** Use pure maple syrup for the best flavor. Imitation maple syrup won't provide the same depth of taste.
- **Consistency:** If the glaze is too thick, you can thin it with a splash of water or additional maple syrup.

Maple-glazed carrots add a sweet and savory element to any meal, making them a perfect side dish for both everyday dinners and special occasions. Enjoy!

Cinnamon Buns

Ingredients:

- **For the Dough:**
    - 1 cup (240 ml) warm milk (110°F or 45°C)
    - 1/4 cup (50 g) granulated sugar
    - 2 1/4 teaspoons (1 packet) active dry yeast
    - 1/2 cup (115 g) unsalted butter, melted
    - 1 large egg
    - 4 cups (480 g) all-purpose flour
    - 1/2 teaspoon salt
- **For the Filling:**
    - 1/2 cup (115 g) unsalted butter, softened
    - 1 cup (200 g) packed brown sugar
    - 2 tablespoons ground cinnamon
- **For the Glaze:**
    - 1 cup (120 g) powdered sugar
    - 2 tablespoons milk
    - 1/2 teaspoon vanilla extract

Instructions:

1. **Prepare the Dough:**
    1. In a small bowl, combine the warm milk and granulated sugar. Sprinkle the yeast on top and let it sit for 5-10 minutes until frothy.
    2. In a large bowl, mix together the melted butter and egg. Add the yeast mixture.
    3. Gradually add the flour and salt to the wet ingredients, mixing until a soft dough forms.
    4. Transfer the dough to a lightly floured surface and knead for about 5-7 minutes, until the dough is smooth and elastic.
    5. Place the dough in a lightly greased bowl, cover with a clean kitchen towel, and let it rise in a warm place for about 1-2 hours, or until doubled in size.
2. **Prepare the Filling:**
    1. In a small bowl, mix together the softened butter, brown sugar, and ground cinnamon until well combined.
3. **Assemble the Cinnamon Buns:**
    1. Preheat your oven to 350°F (175°C).
    2. Once the dough has risen, punch it down and transfer it to a floured surface. Roll it out into a rectangle about 1/4 inch (6 mm) thick.
    3. Spread the cinnamon filling evenly over the dough, leaving a small border around the edges.

    4. Roll the dough up tightly from one edge to the other, forming a log.
    5. Slice the log into 12-15 even pieces.
4. **Bake the Buns:**
    1. Arrange the sliced buns in a greased 9x13 inch (23x33 cm) baking dish or on a parchment-lined baking sheet.
    2. Cover with a clean kitchen towel and let rise for another 30 minutes.
    3. Bake for 20-25 minutes, or until the buns are golden brown and cooked through.
5. **Prepare the Glaze:**
    1. While the buns are baking, whisk together the powdered sugar, milk, and vanilla extract until smooth.
    2. Once the buns are out of the oven, let them cool slightly before drizzling with the glaze.
6. **Serve:**
    1. Serve the cinnamon buns warm or at room temperature, drizzled with the glaze.

Tips:

- **Proofing Yeast:** Make sure the milk is warm, not hot, to avoid killing the yeast. It should be just warm to the touch.
- **Soft Butter:** Use softened butter for the filling to make it easier to spread.
- **Rolling:** When rolling out the dough, try to keep the thickness consistent to ensure even baking.

These cinnamon buns are soft, gooey, and bursting with cinnamon flavor. They make a perfect treat for any occasion or a delightful breakfast to enjoy with a cup of coffee or tea. Enjoy!

Apple Crisp

Ingredients:

- **For the Dough:**
    - 1 cup (240 ml) warm milk (110°F or 45°C)
    - 1/4 cup (50 g) granulated sugar
    - 2 1/4 teaspoons (1 packet) active dry yeast
    - 1/2 cup (115 g) unsalted butter, melted
    - 1 large egg
    - 4 cups (480 g) all-purpose flour
    - 1/2 teaspoon salt
- **For the Filling:**
    - 1/2 cup (115 g) unsalted butter, softened
    - 1 cup (200 g) packed brown sugar
    - 2 tablespoons ground cinnamon
- **For the Glaze:**
    - 1 cup (120 g) powdered sugar
    - 2 tablespoons milk
    - 1/2 teaspoon vanilla extract

Instructions:

1. **Prepare the Dough:**
    1. In a small bowl, combine the warm milk and granulated sugar. Sprinkle the yeast on top and let it sit for 5-10 minutes until frothy.
    2. In a large bowl, mix together the melted butter and egg. Add the yeast mixture.
    3. Gradually add the flour and salt to the wet ingredients, mixing until a soft dough forms.
    4. Transfer the dough to a lightly floured surface and knead for about 5-7 minutes, until the dough is smooth and elastic.
    5. Place the dough in a lightly greased bowl, cover with a clean kitchen towel, and let it rise in a warm place for about 1-2 hours, or until doubled in size.
2. **Prepare the Filling:**
    1. In a small bowl, mix together the softened butter, brown sugar, and ground cinnamon until well combined.
3. **Assemble the Cinnamon Buns:**
    1. Preheat your oven to 350°F (175°C).
    2. Once the dough has risen, punch it down and transfer it to a floured surface. Roll it out into a rectangle about 1/4 inch (6 mm) thick.
    3. Spread the cinnamon filling evenly over the dough, leaving a small border around the edges.

4. Roll the dough up tightly from one edge to the other, forming a log.
   5. Slice the log into 12-15 even pieces.
4. **Bake the Buns:**
   1. Arrange the sliced buns in a greased 9x13 inch (23x33 cm) baking dish or on a parchment-lined baking sheet.
   2. Cover with a clean kitchen towel and let rise for another 30 minutes.
   3. Bake for 20-25 minutes, or until the buns are golden brown and cooked through.
5. **Prepare the Glaze:**
   1. While the buns are baking, whisk together the powdered sugar, milk, and vanilla extract until smooth.
   2. Once the buns are out of the oven, let them cool slightly before drizzling with the glaze.
6. **Serve:**
   1. Serve the cinnamon buns warm or at room temperature, drizzled with the glaze.

Tips:

- **Proofing Yeast:** Make sure the milk is warm, not hot, to avoid killing the yeast. It should be just warm to the touch.
- **Soft Butter:** Use softened butter for the filling to make it easier to spread.
- **Rolling:** When rolling out the dough, try to keep the thickness consistent to ensure even baking.

These cinnamon buns are soft, gooey, and bursting with cinnamon flavor. They make a perfect treat for any occasion or a delightful breakfast to enjoy with a cup of coffee or tea. Enjoy!

Apple Crisp

Ingredients:

- **For the Filling:**
    - 6-7 medium apples (about 3 pounds or 1.4 kg), peeled, cored, and sliced
    - 1/2 cup (100 g) granulated sugar
    - 1 tablespoon lemon juice
    - 1 teaspoon ground cinnamon
    - 1/4 teaspoon ground nutmeg
    - 1/4 teaspoon salt
    - 2 tablespoons all-purpose flour or cornstarch (to thicken)
- **For the Crisp Topping:**
    - 1 cup (90 g) old-fashioned rolled oats
    - 1/2 cup (65 g) all-purpose flour
    - 1/2 cup (100 g) packed brown sugar
    - 1/2 cup (115 g) unsalted butter, cold and cut into small pieces
    - 1/4 teaspoon salt
    - 1/2 cup (50 g) chopped nuts (optional, such as pecans or walnuts)

Instructions:

1. **Prepare the Apples:**
    1. Preheat your oven to 350°F (175°C).
    2. In a large bowl, toss the sliced apples with granulated sugar, lemon juice, ground cinnamon, ground nutmeg, salt, and flour or cornstarch. The flour or cornstarch helps thicken the juices as the apples cook.
2. **Prepare the Topping:**
    1. In a separate bowl, mix together the rolled oats, flour, brown sugar, and salt.
    2. Cut the cold butter into the mixture using a pastry cutter, fork, or your fingers until the mixture resembles coarse crumbs. If using nuts, stir them in at this stage.
3. **Assemble the Crisp:**
    1. Transfer the apple mixture to a 9x13 inch (23x33 cm) baking dish or a similar-sized ovenproof dish.
    2. Evenly sprinkle the crisp topping over the apples.
4. **Bake:**
    1. Bake in the preheated oven for 45-55 minutes, or until the topping is golden brown and the apples are tender and bubbly. The exact baking time may vary depending on your oven and the thickness of the apple slices.
5. **Serve:**
    1. Let the apple crisp cool slightly before serving. It's excellent on its own or with a scoop of vanilla ice cream or a dollop of whipped cream.

Tips:

- **Apple Variety:** Use a mix of sweet and tart apples for the best flavor. Good options include Granny Smith, Honeycrisp, and Fuji.
- **Thickening Agents:** If you prefer a thicker filling, you can add a bit more flour or cornstarch.
- **Crunchy Topping:** For extra crunch, add chopped nuts like pecans or walnuts to the topping.

Apple crisp is a versatile dessert that's easy to adapt and always a crowd-pleaser. Enjoy the warm, comforting flavors and the delightful combination of tender apples and crisp topping!

Beef Pot Roast

Ingredients:

- **For the Roast:**
    - 3 to 4 pounds (1.4 to 1.8 kg) beef chuck roast
    - Salt and freshly ground black pepper, to taste
    - 2 tablespoons olive oil or vegetable oil
    - 1 large onion, chopped
    - 3 cloves garlic, minced
    - 1 cup (240 ml) beef broth
    - 1 cup (240 ml) red wine (optional, you can use additional beef broth if preferred)
    - 2 tablespoons tomato paste
    - 1 tablespoon Worcestershire sauce
    - 2 teaspoons dried thyme
    - 2 teaspoons dried rosemary
    - 2 bay leaves
- **For the Vegetables:**
    - 4 large carrots, peeled and cut into chunks
    - 4 large potatoes, peeled and cut into chunks (Yukon Gold or Russet work well)
    - 2 stalks celery, chopped

Instructions:

1. **Prepare the Beef:**
    1. Pat the beef chuck roast dry with paper towels. Season all sides generously with salt and black pepper.
    2. Heat the olive oil in a large Dutch oven or ovenproof pot over medium-high heat. Sear the beef roast on all sides until browned, about 4-5 minutes per side. Remove the roast from the pot and set aside.
2. **Sauté Aromatics:**
    1. In the same pot, add the chopped onion and cook until softened, about 5 minutes.
    2. Stir in the minced garlic and cook for another minute until fragrant.
3. **Deglaze the Pot:**
    1. Pour in the red wine (if using) and beef broth, scraping up any browned bits from the bottom of the pot with a wooden spoon.
    2. Stir in the tomato paste, Worcestershire sauce, dried thyme, dried rosemary, and bay leaves.
4. **Combine and Cook:**
    1. Return the seared beef roast to the pot, nestling it into the liquid.
    2. Bring the liquid to a simmer, then cover the pot with a lid.

3. Transfer the pot to the preheated oven and roast for about 2.5 to 3 hours, or until the meat is very tender and easily shreds with a fork. Alternatively, you can cook the roast on the stovetop over low heat for the same amount of time.

5. **Add Vegetables:**
    1. About 1 hour before the roast is done, add the carrots, potatoes, and celery to the pot. Make sure the vegetables are submerged in the liquid.
    2. Continue cooking until the vegetables are tender and the roast is fork-tender.
6. **Serve:**
    1. Remove the roast from the pot and let it rest for 10-15 minutes before slicing or shredding.
    2. Discard the bay leaves and adjust seasoning with salt and pepper if needed.
    3. Serve the beef pot roast with the cooked vegetables and spoon some of the flavorful gravy over the top.

Tips:

- **Resting the Meat:** Let the roast rest before slicing to help retain the juices.
- **Gravy:** If you'd like to thicken the gravy, remove the cooked vegetables and roast from the pot, then simmer the liquid until reduced. You can also mix 2 tablespoons of cornstarch with 2 tablespoons of water to create a slurry, then stir it into the simmering liquid to thicken.
- **Slow Cooker:** This recipe can be adapted for a slow cooker. Sear the beef and sauté the aromatics, then transfer everything to a slow cooker and cook on low for 8-10 hours or high for 4-5 hours.

Beef pot roast is a comforting and flavorful dish that's perfect for family dinners or special occasions. Enjoy the rich, savory flavors and tender meat!

Turkey with Cranberry Sauce

Ingredients:

- **For the Turkey:**
    - 12 to 14 pounds (5.4 to 6.4 kg) whole turkey, thawed if frozen
    - 1/2 cup (115 g) unsalted butter, melted
    - Salt and freshly ground black pepper
    - 1 tablespoon dried thyme
    - 1 tablespoon dried rosemary
    - 1 tablespoon dried sage (or 2 tablespoons fresh sage, chopped)
    - 1 large onion, quartered
    - 2-3 cloves garlic, smashed
    - 1 lemon, quartered
    - 1-2 cups (240-480 ml) chicken or turkey broth

Instructions:

1. **Preheat Oven:**
    - Preheat your oven to 325°F (165°C).
2. **Prepare the Turkey:**
    - Remove the turkey giblets and neck from the cavity. Pat the turkey dry with paper towels.
    - Rub the entire turkey with melted butter. Season generously with salt, pepper, dried thyme, rosemary, and sage.
    - Stuff the cavity with the quartered onion, garlic, and lemon.
3. **Roast the Turkey:**
    - Place the turkey breast side up on a rack in a roasting pan.
    - Tent the turkey loosely with aluminum foil to prevent over-browning.
    - Roast in the preheated oven. As a general guideline, cook the turkey for about 15 minutes per pound. For a 12-14 pound turkey, this will be approximately 3 to 3.5 hours.
    - Baste the turkey with the pan juices every 45 minutes. Remove the foil during the last 45 minutes to allow the skin to crisp up.
4. **Check Doneness:**
    - The turkey is done when the internal temperature reaches 165°F (74°C) in the thickest part of the thigh, and the juices run clear.
    - Let the turkey rest for 20-30 minutes before carving. This helps the juices redistribute.

Cranberry Sauce

Ingredients:

- 12 ounces (340 g) fresh or frozen cranberries
- 1 cup (200 g) granulated sugar
- 1 cup (240 ml) water
- 1/2 cup (120 ml) orange juice
- 1/4 teaspoon ground cinnamon
- 1/4 teaspoon ground nutmeg
- 1 tablespoon grated orange zest (optional)

Instructions:

1. **Cook the Cranberries:**
   - In a medium saucepan, combine the sugar, water, and orange juice. Bring to a boil, stirring occasionally.
   - Add the cranberries and return to a boil. Reduce heat and simmer for about 10 minutes, or until the cranberries burst and the sauce thickens. Stir occasionally.
2. **Add Spices:**
   - Stir in the ground cinnamon, nutmeg, and orange zest (if using).
3. **Cool and Serve:**
   - Remove from heat and let the cranberry sauce cool to room temperature. It will thicken further as it cools.
   - Transfer to a serving dish and refrigerate until ready to serve.

Serving Suggestions:

- Serve slices of roasted turkey with a generous spoonful of cranberry sauce on the side.
- The cranberry sauce also pairs well with stuffing, mashed potatoes, and other traditional sides.

Tips:

- **Resting the Turkey:** Allowing the turkey to rest before carving helps keep it juicy and tender.
- **Flavor Variations:** You can add other ingredients to the cranberry sauce, like chopped nuts, diced apples, or a splash of brandy, to enhance the flavor.

Enjoy your delicious roast turkey with cranberry sauce, a perfect centerpiece for any festive meal!

Fish Tacos

Ingredients:

- **For the Fish:**
    - 1 pound (450 g) firm white fish (such as cod, tilapia, or mahi-mahi), cut into strips or bite-sized pieces
    - 1 cup all-purpose flour
    - 1 teaspoon paprika
    - 1/2 teaspoon garlic powder
    - 1/2 teaspoon onion powder
    - 1/2 teaspoon cumin
    - 1/2 teaspoon salt
    - 1/4 teaspoon black pepper
    - 1/2 teaspoon cayenne pepper (optional, for heat)
    - 1 cup buttermilk (or regular milk)
    - Vegetable oil for frying
- **For the Toppings:**
    - 1 cup shredded cabbage (green, red, or a mix)
    - 1 medium carrot, peeled and shredded
    - 1 avocado, sliced
    - 1/2 red onion, thinly sliced
    - Fresh cilantro leaves, for garnish
    - Lime wedges, for serving
- **For the Sauce:**
    - 1/2 cup mayonnaise
    - 2 tablespoons sour cream or Greek yogurt
    - 1 tablespoon lime juice
    - 1 teaspoon honey or agave syrup
    - 1 teaspoon hot sauce (optional)
    - Salt and pepper to taste
- **For Serving:**
    - Corn or flour tortillas, warmed

Instructions:

1. **Prepare the Sauce:**
    1. In a small bowl, whisk together the mayonnaise, sour cream or Greek yogurt, lime juice, honey or agave syrup, and hot sauce (if using).
    2. Season with salt and pepper to taste. Set aside.
2. **Prepare the Fish:**

1. In a medium bowl, mix the flour, paprika, garlic powder, onion powder, cumin, salt, black pepper, and cayenne pepper (if using).
2. Pour the buttermilk into a separate bowl.
3. Dip the fish pieces into the buttermilk, allowing excess to drip off, then dredge them in the seasoned flour mixture, pressing lightly to adhere.

3. **Fry the Fish:**
    1. Heat about 1/2 inch (1.25 cm) of vegetable oil in a large skillet over medium-high heat until shimmering.
    2. Fry the fish in batches, without crowding the pan, for 3-4 minutes per side, or until golden brown and crispy. Remove the fish and drain on paper towels.
4. **Prepare the Toppings:**
    1. In a bowl, toss the shredded cabbage and carrot together.
    2. Slice the avocado and thinly slice the red onion.
5. **Assemble the Tacos:**
    1. Warm the tortillas in a dry skillet or on a griddle until soft and pliable.
    2. Spread a bit of the sauce on each tortilla.
    3. Top with a few pieces of fried fish.
    4. Add a handful of the cabbage and carrot mixture.
    5. Top with avocado slices, red onion, and a sprinkle of fresh cilantro.
6. **Serve:**
    1. Serve the tacos immediately with lime wedges on the side for squeezing over the top.

Tips:

- **Tortilla Choice:** Corn tortillas are traditional for fish tacos, but flour tortillas work well too if you prefer them.
- **Crispy Fish:** For extra crispy fish, make sure the oil is hot enough before adding the fish and avoid overcrowding the pan.
- **Customizing:** Feel free to customize your toppings with ingredients like diced tomatoes, sliced jalapeños, or a sprinkle of feta cheese.

Fish tacos are a fresh and flavorful meal that's sure to be a hit. Enjoy the combination of crispy fish, creamy sauce, and fresh vegetables in every bite!

Maple Mustard Pork Chops

Ingredients:

- **For the Pork Chops:**
    - 4 bone-in or boneless pork chops (about 1-inch thick)
    - Salt and freshly ground black pepper
    - 2 tablespoons olive oil
- **For the Maple Mustard Sauce:**
    - 1/4 cup (60 ml) pure maple syrup
    - 2 tablespoons Dijon mustard
    - 1 tablespoon whole-grain mustard
    - 1 tablespoon apple cider vinegar or white wine vinegar
    - 1 teaspoon minced garlic
    - 1 teaspoon dried thyme or 1 tablespoon fresh thyme leaves
    - 1/2 teaspoon dried rosemary (optional)
    - Salt and freshly ground black pepper to taste

Instructions:

1. **Prepare the Pork Chops:**
    1. Season both sides of the pork chops with salt and freshly ground black pepper.
    2. Heat olive oil in a large skillet over medium-high heat.
2. **Cook the Pork Chops:**
    1. Add the pork chops to the hot skillet and cook for about 4-5 minutes per side, or until the chops are browned and cooked through. The internal temperature should reach 145°F (63°C).
    2. Remove the pork chops from the skillet and set aside on a plate to rest.
3. **Make the Maple Mustard Sauce:**
    1. In the same skillet, reduce the heat to medium.
    2. Add the minced garlic and cook for about 30 seconds until fragrant.
    3. Stir in the maple syrup, Dijon mustard, whole-grain mustard, vinegar, thyme, and rosemary (if using).
    4. Bring the sauce to a simmer, scraping up any browned bits from the bottom of the skillet.
    5. Simmer for about 2-3 minutes, or until the sauce has thickened slightly. Adjust seasoning with salt and pepper to taste.
4. **Finish the Dish:**
    1. Return the pork chops to the skillet, spooning the sauce over them.
    2. Simmer for an additional 1-2 minutes, allowing the pork chops to soak up some of the sauce.
5. **Serve:**

1. Transfer the pork chops to serving plates and spoon additional sauce over the top.
2. Garnish with extra fresh thyme if desired.

Serving Suggestions:

- **Side Dishes:** These pork chops pair well with a variety of sides, including roasted vegetables, mashed potatoes, or a simple green salad.
- **Vegetables:** Consider serving with steamed green beans, sautéed spinach, or a medley of roasted root vegetables for a complete meal.

Tips:

- **Resting the Meat:** Letting the pork chops rest for a few minutes after cooking helps keep them juicy.
- **Thickening the Sauce:** If you prefer a thicker sauce, simmer it a bit longer or mix a small amount of cornstarch with water and stir it into the sauce.
- **Maple Syrup:** Use pure maple syrup for the best flavor. Imitation maple syrup won't provide the same depth.

Maple mustard pork chops offer a delightful combination of sweet and tangy flavors that are sure to please. Enjoy this easy and delicious meal!

Scalloped Potatoes

Ingredients:

- **For the Potatoes:**
    - 2 pounds (900 g) russet or Yukon Gold potatoes, peeled and thinly sliced (about 1/8 inch or 3 mm thick)
    - 1 large onion, finely chopped (optional)
- **For the Sauce:**
    - 4 tablespoons (60 g) unsalted butter
    - 1/4 cup (30 g) all-purpose flour
    - 2 cups (480 ml) whole milk
    - 1 cup (240 ml) heavy cream
    - 2 cups (200 g) shredded sharp cheddar cheese
    - 1 teaspoon salt
    - 1/2 teaspoon freshly ground black pepper
    - 1/4 teaspoon ground nutmeg (optional)
    - 1/2 teaspoon dried thyme or rosemary (optional)
    - 1 cup (100 g) grated Parmesan cheese (for topping)

Instructions:

1. **Preheat Oven:**
    - Preheat your oven to 375°F (190°C).
2. **Prepare the Potatoes:**
    - Peel and thinly slice the potatoes. If you have a mandoline slicer, it can help achieve uniform slices.
    - Place the sliced potatoes in a large bowl of cold water to prevent browning. Drain and pat dry with paper towels before using.
3. **Make the Sauce:**
    - In a medium saucepan, melt the butter over medium heat.
    - Stir in the flour and cook, whisking constantly, for about 1-2 minutes until the mixture is bubbly and golden but not browned (this is the roux).
    - Gradually whisk in the milk and heavy cream, ensuring there are no lumps. Continue to cook, whisking frequently, until the mixture thickens and begins to simmer, about 5-7 minutes.
    - Remove the saucepan from heat and stir in the shredded cheddar cheese until melted and smooth.
    - Season with salt, black pepper, nutmeg, and thyme or rosemary if using.
4. **Assemble the Dish:**
    - Grease a 9x13 inch (23x33 cm) baking dish or a similar-sized ovenproof dish.

- Layer half of the sliced potatoes evenly in the bottom of the dish. If using, sprinkle the layer with some of the finely chopped onion.
- Pour half of the cheese sauce over the potatoes.
- Repeat with the remaining potatoes and cheese sauce.

5. **Add Topping:**
    - Sprinkle the grated Parmesan cheese evenly over the top.
6. **Bake:**
    - Cover the dish with aluminum foil and bake in the preheated oven for 45 minutes.
    - Remove the foil and bake for an additional 20-25 minutes, or until the top is golden brown and the potatoes are tender. You can test the doneness by inserting a knife into the center; it should go through easily.
7. **Cool and Serve:**
    - Let the scalloped potatoes cool for a few minutes before serving. This helps the sauce thicken slightly and makes serving easier.

Tips:

- **Potato Variety:** Russet potatoes are starchy and work well for a creamy texture, while Yukon Golds are slightly waxy and will hold their shape better.
- **Cheese:** Feel free to mix different types of cheese for a richer flavor. Gruyère, Monterey Jack, or Gouda can be excellent additions.
- **Make Ahead:** You can prepare scalloped potatoes a day in advance. Just assemble the dish and refrigerate, then bake it the next day. You might need to add a few extra minutes to the baking time if cooking straight from the refrigerator.

Scalloped potatoes are a classic comfort food that pairs beautifully with a variety of main dishes, from roast meats to hearty casseroles. Enjoy this creamy and delicious side!

Blackberry Crisp

Ingredients:

- **For the Filling:**
    - 4 cups (500 g) fresh or frozen blackberries
    - 1/2 cup (100 g) granulated sugar
    - 1 tablespoon lemon juice
    - 2 tablespoons all-purpose flour or cornstarch (to thicken)
    - 1/2 teaspoon vanilla extract (optional)
    - 1/4 teaspoon ground cinnamon (optional)
- **For the Crisp Topping:**
    - 1 cup (90 g) old-fashioned rolled oats
    - 1/2 cup (65 g) all-purpose flour
    - 1/2 cup (100 g) packed brown sugar
    - 1/2 cup (115 g) unsalted butter, cold and cut into small pieces
    - 1/4 teaspoon salt
    - 1/2 cup (50 g) chopped nuts (optional, such as pecans or walnuts)

Instructions:

1. **Preheat Oven:**
    - Preheat your oven to 350°F (175°C).
2. **Prepare the Filling:**
    - In a large bowl, gently toss the blackberries with granulated sugar, lemon juice, flour or cornstarch, vanilla extract (if using), and ground cinnamon (if using).
    - Transfer the mixture to a 9x13 inch (23x33 cm) baking dish or a similar-sized ovenproof dish.
3. **Prepare the Crisp Topping:**
    - In a separate bowl, mix together the rolled oats, flour, brown sugar, and salt.
    - Cut the cold butter into the mixture using a pastry cutter, fork, or your fingers until the mixture resembles coarse crumbs. If you're adding nuts, stir them in now.
4. **Assemble the Crisp:**
    - Evenly sprinkle the crisp topping over the blackberry filling.
5. **Bake:**
    - Bake in the preheated oven for 45-55 minutes, or until the topping is golden brown and the blackberry filling is bubbling. The exact baking time may vary depending on your oven and the thickness of the filling.
6. **Cool and Serve:**
    - Let the blackberry crisp cool slightly before serving. This helps the filling set a bit, making it easier to scoop.

Serving Suggestions:

- **A La Mode:** Serve warm with a scoop of vanilla ice cream or a dollop of whipped cream for an extra treat.
- **Plain:** It's also delicious on its own as a simple and comforting dessert.

Tips:

- **Berry Variations:** Feel free to mix in other berries like blueberries, raspberries, or strawberries with the blackberries for a mixed berry crisp.
- **Thickening Agent:** Adjust the amount of flour or cornstarch based on how juicy your berries are. If using frozen berries, you may need a bit more thickening.

Blackberry crisp is a versatile and easy dessert that highlights the natural sweetness of blackberries and pairs beautifully with a variety of toppings. Enjoy this sweet and comforting treat!

Gingerbread Cookies

Ingredients:

- **For the Cookies:**
    - 3 1/4 cups (400 g) all-purpose flour
    - 1/2 teaspoon baking soda
    - 1 tablespoon ground ginger
    - 1 tablespoon ground cinnamon
    - 1/2 teaspoon ground cloves
    - 1/4 teaspoon salt
    - 1/2 cup (115 g) unsalted butter, at room temperature
    - 1/2 cup (100 g) granulated sugar
    - 1/2 cup (160 g) dark molasses or blackstrap molasses
    - 1 large egg
    - 1 tablespoon fresh grated ginger (optional, for extra spice)
- **For the Royal Icing (Optional, for Decorating):**
    - 2 large egg whites
    - 4 cups (450 g) powdered sugar, sifted
    - 1/2 teaspoon lemon juice or white vinegar
    - Food coloring (optional)

Instructions:

1. **Prepare the Dough:**
    1. In a medium bowl, whisk together the flour, baking soda, ginger, cinnamon, cloves, and salt.
    2. In a large bowl, beat the butter and granulated sugar together until light and fluffy, about 3-4 minutes.
    3. Beat in the molasses, egg, and fresh grated ginger (if using) until well combined.
    4. Gradually add the dry ingredients to the wet ingredients, mixing until just combined. The dough will be thick.
2. **Chill the Dough:**
    1. Divide the dough into two equal portions, flatten them into discs, and wrap in plastic wrap.
    2. Refrigerate for at least 1 hour, or until firm. Chilling helps the cookies hold their shape while baking.
3. **Preheat Oven:**
    1. Preheat your oven to 350°F (175°C).
4. **Roll and Cut the Dough:**
    1. On a lightly floured surface, roll out one portion of dough to about 1/4 inch (6 mm) thick.

2. Use cookie cutters to cut out shapes and place them on a parchment-lined baking sheet.
   3. Gather and reroll scraps as needed.
5. **Bake:**
   1. Bake the cookies in the preheated oven for 8-10 minutes, or until the edges are just starting to darken.
   2. Cool on the baking sheets for a few minutes before transferring to a wire rack to cool completely.
6. **Decorate (Optional):**
   1. **Prepare the Royal Icing:**
      - In a large bowl, beat the egg whites until frothy. Gradually add the sifted powdered sugar and lemon juice or vinegar, beating until stiff peaks form.
      - If using food coloring, divide the icing into separate bowls and tint with gel food colors.
   2. **Decorate the Cookies:**
      - Use piping bags or a small spoon to decorate the cooled cookies with the royal icing. You can create intricate designs, outlines, and patterns.
      - Let the decorated cookies sit at room temperature until the icing is completely dry, which can take several hours.

Tips:

- **Rolling the Dough:** If the dough is too sticky, dust it lightly with flour. If it's too stiff, let it sit at room temperature for a few minutes to soften.
- **Icing Consistency:** For decorating, the royal icing should be thick enough to hold its shape but not so thick that it's difficult to pipe. Adjust with a bit of water if needed.
- **Storage:** Store cooled, undecorated cookies in an airtight container at room temperature for up to one week. Decorated cookies can be stored in the same manner once the icing is dry.

Gingerbread cookies are not only a tasty treat but also a fun and festive activity to enjoy during the holidays. Have fun decorating and sharing them with loved ones!

Maple Walnut Granola

Ingredients:

- **For the Granola:**
    - 3 cups (240 g) old-fashioned rolled oats
    - 1 cup (120 g) chopped walnuts
    - 1/2 cup (50 g) slivered almonds (optional)
    - 1/4 cup (35 g) unsweetened shredded coconut (optional)
    - 1/4 cup (60 ml) pure maple syrup
    - 1/4 cup (60 ml) coconut oil or vegetable oil
    - 1/4 cup (50 g) packed brown sugar
    - 1/2 teaspoon ground cinnamon
    - 1/4 teaspoon salt
    - 1/2 cup (80 g) dried fruit (such as cranberries, raisins, or apricots), chopped if large

Instructions:

1. **Preheat Oven:**
    - Preheat your oven to 350°F (175°C). Line a large baking sheet with parchment paper or a silicone baking mat.
2. **Prepare the Granola Mixture:**
    - In a large bowl, combine the rolled oats, chopped walnuts, slivered almonds (if using), and shredded coconut (if using).
3. **Make the Maple Mixture:**
    - In a small saucepan over medium heat, combine the maple syrup, coconut oil, brown sugar, ground cinnamon, and salt. Stir until the mixture is smooth and the sugar has dissolved. Remove from heat.
4. **Combine and Coat:**
    - Pour the maple mixture over the oat and nut mixture. Stir well until all the dry ingredients are evenly coated.
5. **Bake:**
    - Spread the granola mixture evenly on the prepared baking sheet.
    - Bake in the preheated oven for 20-25 minutes, stirring halfway through, until the granola is golden brown and crisp. Keep a close eye on it toward the end to prevent burning.
6. **Cool and Add Dried Fruit:**
    - Remove from the oven and let the granola cool completely on the baking sheet. It will become crunchier as it cools.
    - Once cooled, stir in the dried fruit.
7. **Store:**

- Transfer the granola to an airtight container. It will keep at room temperature for up to 2 weeks or in the refrigerator for up to 1 month.

Serving Suggestions:

- **With Yogurt:** Serve over Greek yogurt with fresh fruit for a delicious breakfast or snack.
- **With Milk:** Enjoy with milk or a dairy-free alternative for a classic granola and milk combination.
- **On Its Own:** It's also great as a crunchy snack right out of the container.

Tips:

- **Customization:** Feel free to customize your granola by adding seeds (like chia or flaxseeds), other nuts (such as pecans or cashews), or different spices (like nutmeg or allspice).
- **Clumps:** For clumpier granola, press the mixture down with a spatula before baking and avoid stirring too frequently while baking.

Maple walnut granola is a versatile and wholesome option that's perfect for breakfast or a snack. Enjoy making and savoring your homemade granola!

Rhubarb Pie

Ingredients:

- **For the Pie Crust:**
    - 2 1/2 cups (315 g) all-purpose flour
    - 1 cup (225 g) unsalted butter, cold and cut into small pieces
    - 1/4 cup (50 g) granulated sugar
    - 1/4 teaspoon salt
    - 4-6 tablespoons ice water
- **For the Rhubarb Filling:**
    - 4 cups (500 g) fresh rhubarb, cut into 1/2-inch (1.25 cm) pieces
    - 1 1/4 cups (250 g) granulated sugar
    - 1/4 cup (30 g) cornstarch
    - 1/4 teaspoon salt
    - 1 teaspoon vanilla extract (optional)
    - 1 tablespoon lemon juice (optional)
    - 1/2 teaspoon ground cinnamon (optional)
- **For the Topping (Optional):**
    - 1 tablespoon butter, cut into small pieces
    - 1 tablespoon granulated sugar (for sprinkling on top)

Instructions:

1. **Prepare the Pie Crust:**
    - In a large bowl, combine the flour, granulated sugar, and salt.
    - Add the cold butter pieces and use a pastry cutter, fork, or your fingers to work the butter into the flour mixture until it resembles coarse crumbs with pea-sized pieces of butter.
    - Gradually add ice water, 1 tablespoon at a time, mixing until the dough just comes together. You may not need all the water.
    - Divide the dough in half, shape into discs, wrap in plastic wrap, and refrigerate for at least 1 hour.
2. **Prepare the Filling:**
    - In a large bowl, combine the rhubarb, granulated sugar, cornstarch, salt, vanilla extract (if using), lemon juice (if using), and ground cinnamon (if using). Mix well to coat the rhubarb evenly. Set aside.
3. **Assemble the Pie:**
    - Preheat your oven to 400°F (200°C).
    - On a lightly floured surface, roll out one disc of dough to fit a 9-inch (23 cm) pie dish. Transfer the rolled dough to the dish and press it into the bottom and sides. Trim any excess dough hanging over the edges.

- Pour the rhubarb filling into the pie crust and spread it evenly.
- Roll out the second disc of dough and place it over the filling. You can either use it as a whole top crust or cut it into strips to make a lattice crust. If using a whole top crust, cut a few slits in the top to allow steam to escape. If making a lattice crust, weave the strips over the filling and trim the edges, pressing to seal. Crimp the edges to seal.
- Dot the top crust with small pieces of butter and sprinkle with granulated sugar.

4. **Bake:**
   - Place the pie on a baking sheet to catch any drips.
   - Bake in the preheated oven for 45-55 minutes, or until the crust is golden brown and the filling is bubbly.
   - If the edges of the crust start to brown too quickly, cover them with aluminum foil.

5. **Cool:**
   - Allow the pie to cool on a wire rack for at least 2 hours before slicing. This helps the filling set and makes it easier to slice.

Tips:

- **Rhubarb Preparation:** Make sure to use fresh rhubarb. If using frozen rhubarb, thaw and drain it thoroughly to avoid excess moisture in the pie.
- **Pie Crust:** For a flakier crust, ensure the butter is cold and handle the dough as little as possible to avoid warming it up.
- **Sweetness Level:** Adjust the amount of sugar in the filling to your taste, especially if your rhubarb is very tart.

Rhubarb pie is a delightful and classic dessert with a perfect balance of tart and sweet. Enjoy this homemade pie as a treat for special occasions or simply as a comforting dessert!

Sour Cherry Soup

Ingredients:

- **For the Soup:**
    - 4 cups (950 ml) pitted sour cherries (fresh or frozen)
    - 4 cups (950 ml) water
    - 1 cup (200 g) granulated sugar (adjust to taste)
    - 1 tablespoon lemon juice
    - 1/2 teaspoon ground cinnamon (optional)
    - 1/4 teaspoon ground cloves (optional)
    - 1/4 cup (60 ml) red wine (optional, for extra depth)
    - 1 tablespoon cornstarch or arrowroot powder (optional, for thickening)
- **For Garnish (Optional):**
    - Fresh mint leaves
    - Whipped cream or sour cream
    - Crumbled cookies or biscotti
    - Fresh cherries

Instructions:

1. **Prepare the Cherries:**
    - If using fresh cherries, wash and pit them. If using frozen cherries, thaw them and drain excess liquid.
2. **Cook the Soup:**
    - In a large pot, combine the cherries and water. Bring to a boil over medium-high heat.
    - Reduce the heat and simmer for about 10-15 minutes, until the cherries are soft and the flavors have melded.
    - Remove from heat and let the mixture cool slightly.
3. **Blend the Soup:**
    - Use an immersion blender to puree the mixture until smooth. Alternatively, you can transfer it in batches to a blender.
    - If you prefer a chunkier texture, blend only part of the mixture or use a potato masher for a more rustic texture.
4. **Sweeten and Season:**
    - Return the blended cherry mixture to the pot. Stir in the granulated sugar, lemon juice, and optional spices (cinnamon and cloves).
    - If you'd like a thicker soup, mix the cornstarch or arrowroot powder with a few tablespoons of cold water to form a slurry, then stir it into the soup. Heat gently, stirring constantly, until the soup thickens slightly.
5. **Add Wine (Optional):**

- Stir in the red wine if using. This adds a complex flavor but is optional.
6. **Chill the Soup:**
   - Allow the soup to cool to room temperature, then cover and refrigerate for at least 2 hours or until thoroughly chilled.
7. **Serve:**
   - Serve the chilled soup in bowls or cups. Garnish with fresh mint leaves, a dollop of whipped cream or sour cream, crumbled cookies, or fresh cherries, if desired.

Tips:

- **Adjust Sweetness:** Depending on the tartness of your cherries, you may need to adjust the amount of sugar. Taste the soup before refrigerating and add more sugar if necessary.
- **Texture:** For a smooth and refined texture, strain the soup through a fine-mesh sieve after blending to remove any remaining solids.

Sour cherry soup is a delightful and refreshing dish that offers a unique twist on traditional soups. Enjoy it chilled as a light appetizer or a light dessert!

BBQ Ribs

Ingredients:

- **For the Ribs:**
    - 2 racks of baby back ribs or spare ribs (about 4 pounds or 1.8 kg total)
    - 1 tablespoon olive oil
    - 1/2 cup (125 ml) apple cider vinegar
    - 1/4 cup (60 ml) water
- **For the Dry Rub:**
    - 1/4 cup (50 g) brown sugar
    - 1 tablespoon paprika
    - 1 tablespoon ground cumin
    - 1 tablespoon garlic powder
    - 1 tablespoon onion powder
    - 1 teaspoon black pepper
    - 1 teaspoon salt
    - 1 teaspoon chili powder (optional for extra heat)
    - 1/2 teaspoon cayenne pepper (optional for extra heat)
- **For the BBQ Sauce:**
    - 1 cup (240 ml) BBQ sauce (store-bought or homemade; see recipe below for homemade)
    - 2 tablespoons apple cider vinegar
    - 1 tablespoon honey or brown sugar (optional for extra sweetness)

Instructions:

1. **Prepare the Ribs:**
    - **Remove the Membrane:** Place the ribs, bone-side up, on a cutting board. Use a knife to carefully loosen and remove the thin membrane from the back of the ribs. This helps the rub and sauce penetrate better.
    - **Season:** Rub the ribs with olive oil, then apply a generous amount of the dry rub on both sides, pressing it into the meat.
2. **Cook the Ribs:**
    - **Grill Method:**
        1. Preheat your grill to medium heat (about 300-325°F or 150-165°C).
        2. Set up a two-zone cooking area: one side of the grill for direct heat and the other for indirect heat.
        3. Place the ribs on the indirect heat side, bone-side down. Cover and cook for 1.5 to 2 hours, maintaining the grill temperature.
        4. Baste the ribs with a mixture of apple cider vinegar and water every 30 minutes to keep them moist.

5. During the last 30 minutes, move the ribs to the direct heat side and brush with BBQ sauce, turning and basting frequently to caramelize the sauce.
- **Oven Method:**
  1. Preheat your oven to 300°F (150°C).
  2. Place the ribs on a large piece of aluminum foil, bone-side down. Wrap tightly in foil.
  3. Place the wrapped ribs on a baking sheet and bake for 2.5 to 3 hours.
  4. Remove the ribs from the oven and discard the foil. Brush the ribs with BBQ sauce.
  5. Place the ribs under a broiler or on a hot grill for 5-10 minutes to caramelize the sauce, watching closely to avoid burning.
- **Smoker Method:**
  1. Preheat your smoker to 225°F (110°C).
  2. Smoke the ribs for 5-6 hours, maintaining a steady temperature and smoking with your choice of wood (like hickory or applewood).
  3. Baste with a mixture of apple cider vinegar and water every hour.
  4. During the last 30 minutes, brush with BBQ sauce and continue to smoke.

3. **Rest and Serve:**
   - Once cooked, let the ribs rest for 10 minutes before slicing between the bones.
   - Serve with additional BBQ sauce on the side if desired.

Homemade BBQ Sauce:

- **Ingredients:**
  1. 1 cup (240 ml) ketchup
  2. 1/2 cup (120 ml) apple cider vinegar
  3. 1/4 cup (60 ml) honey or brown sugar
  4. 1 tablespoon Worcestershire sauce
  5. 1 tablespoon smoked paprika
  6. 1 teaspoon garlic powder
  7. 1 teaspoon onion powder
  8. Salt and pepper to taste
- **Instructions:**
  1. In a saucepan, combine all ingredients.
  2. Bring to a simmer over medium heat, stirring frequently.
  3. Reduce heat and simmer for 10-15 minutes until thickened.
  4. Let cool before using.

Tips:

- **Rib Types:** Baby back ribs are more tender and leaner, while spare ribs are meatier and have more fat, which makes them juicier but can be a bit tougher.
- **Marinating:** For extra flavor, you can marinate the ribs with the dry rub overnight in the refrigerator.

- **Sauce Application:** Apply the BBQ sauce towards the end of cooking to avoid burning the sugars in the sauce.

Enjoy your delicious BBQ ribs with classic sides like coleslaw, baked beans, or corn on the cob!

Vegetarian Shepherd's Pie

Ingredients:

- **For the Mashed Potatoes:**
    - 2 pounds (900 g) potatoes (such as Russet or Yukon Gold), peeled and cubed
    - 1/2 cup (120 ml) milk or plant-based milk
    - 1/4 cup (60 g) unsalted butter or plant-based butter
    - Salt and pepper to taste
- **For the Filling:**
    - 2 tablespoons olive oil
    - 1 onion, finely chopped
    - 2 cloves garlic, minced
    - 2 carrots, diced
    - 2 celery stalks, diced
    - 1 cup (150 g) mushrooms, diced
    - 1 cup (200 g) dried green or brown lentils, rinsed
    - 1 1/2 cups (375 ml) vegetable broth
    - 1 tablespoon tomato paste
    - 1 tablespoon soy sauce or tamari
    - 1 teaspoon dried thyme
    - 1 teaspoon dried rosemary
    - 1/2 cup (75 g) frozen peas
    - 1/2 cup (75 g) corn kernels (optional)
    - Salt and pepper to taste

Instructions:

1. **Prepare the Mashed Potatoes:**
    - Place the peeled and cubed potatoes in a large pot and cover with cold water. Add a pinch of salt.
    - Bring to a boil over high heat. Reduce heat and simmer until potatoes are tender, about 15-20 minutes.
    - Drain the potatoes and return them to the pot. Mash with a potato masher or use a ricer for a smoother texture.
    - Stir in the milk and butter until creamy. Season with salt and pepper to taste. Set aside.
2. **Prepare the Filling:**
    - Heat olive oil in a large skillet or saucepan over medium heat.
    - Add the onion and garlic, and sauté until the onion is translucent, about 3-4 minutes.

- Add the carrots, celery, and mushrooms, and cook until the vegetables are softened, about 5-7 minutes.
- Stir in the lentils, vegetable broth, tomato paste, soy sauce, thyme, and rosemary.
- Bring to a boil, then reduce heat to low. Cover and simmer until the lentils are tender and most of the liquid is absorbed, about 25-30 minutes. Stir occasionally.
- Add the frozen peas and corn (if using) and cook for an additional 5 minutes. Season with salt and pepper to taste.

3. **Assemble the Shepherd's Pie:**
    - Preheat your oven to 375°F (190°C).
    - Spoon the lentil and vegetable filling into a baking dish, spreading it evenly.
    - Top with the mashed potatoes, spreading them out with a spatula to cover the filling completely. You can use a fork to create a pattern on top if desired.

4. **Bake:**
    - Bake in the preheated oven for 25-30 minutes, or until the top is lightly browned and the filling is bubbling.
    - If you want a more golden top, you can place the pie under the broiler for a few minutes, but watch it closely to avoid burning.

5. **Cool and Serve:**
    - Let the shepherd's pie cool for a few minutes before serving. This allows the filling to set and makes it easier to serve.

Tips:

- **Lentils:** Green or brown lentils work best for this recipe as they hold their shape well. Red lentils tend to become mushy.
- **Vegetable Variations:** Feel free to add other vegetables like bell peppers, parsnips, or sweet potatoes to the filling.
- **Seasoning:** Adjust the seasoning to your taste. You can also add a splash of balsamic vinegar or a teaspoon of smoked paprika for extra flavor.

Vegetarian shepherd's pie is a comforting and nutritious meal that's perfect for family dinners or meal prep. Enjoy it with a side salad or steamed greens for a complete meal!

Lemon Curd Tarts

Ingredients:

- **For the Tart Shells:**
    - 1 1/2 cups (190 g) all-purpose flour
    - 1/2 cup (50 g) powdered sugar
    - 1/2 cup (115 g) unsalted butter, cold and cut into small pieces
    - 1 large egg yolk
    - 1-2 tablespoons ice water (if needed)
- **For the Lemon Curd:**
    - 1/2 cup (120 ml) fresh lemon juice (about 2-3 lemons)
    - 1 tablespoon lemon zest (from 1-2 lemons)
    - 1/2 cup (100 g) granulated sugar
    - 3 large eggs
    - 1/4 cup (60 g) unsalted butter, cut into small pieces
    - Pinch of salt

Instructions:

1. **Prepare the Tart Shells:**
    - **Make the Dough:**
        - In a large bowl, whisk together the flour and powdered sugar.
        - Add the cold butter pieces. Use a pastry cutter, fork, or your fingers to work the butter into the flour mixture until it resembles coarse crumbs.
        - Add the egg yolk and mix until combined. If the dough is too dry, add ice water, a little at a time, until it comes together.
    - **Chill the Dough:**
        - Form the dough into a disk, wrap it in plastic wrap, and refrigerate for at least 1 hour.
    - **Roll and Cut the Dough:**
        - Preheat your oven to 375°F (190°C).
        - On a lightly floured surface, roll out the dough to about 1/8 inch (3 mm) thick.
        - Cut the dough into circles slightly larger than the diameter of your tart pans (about 3-4 inches or 8-10 cm).
        - Press the dough into the tart pans, trimming any excess. Prick the bottoms with a fork to prevent bubbling.
    - **Blind Bake the Tart Shells:**
        - Line each tart shell with parchment paper and fill with pie weights or dried beans.

- Bake in the preheated oven for 10 minutes. Remove the parchment and weights and bake for an additional 5 minutes, or until the shells are lightly golden.
- Allow to cool completely on a wire rack.

2. **Prepare the Lemon Curd:**
    - **Combine Ingredients:**
        - In a medium heatproof bowl, whisk together the lemon juice, lemon zest, sugar, and eggs.
    - **Cook the Curd:**
        - Place the bowl over a pot of simmering water (double boiler method), making sure the bottom of the bowl doesn't touch the water.
        - Cook, whisking constantly, until the mixture thickens and reaches 170°F (77°C) on a kitchen thermometer. This should take about 8-10 minutes.
    - **Finish the Curd:**
        - Remove from heat and stir in the butter until melted and smooth.
        - Strain the lemon curd through a fine-mesh sieve into a clean bowl to remove any bits of cooked egg or zest.
        - Allow the curd to cool to room temperature, then cover and refrigerate until fully chilled and set.

3. **Assemble the Tarts:**
    - Spoon or pipe the chilled lemon curd into the cooled tart shells.
    - Smooth the tops with a spatula or the back of a spoon.

4. **Garnish and Serve:**
    - Garnish with additional lemon zest, a dusting of powdered sugar, or fresh berries if desired.
    - Serve chilled.

Tips:

- **Tart Pans:** If you don't have tart pans, you can use a muffin tin or make mini tarts with a mini muffin tin.
- **Preventing Soggy Bottoms:** Ensure the tart shells are fully cooled before adding the curd to prevent sogginess.
- **Storage:** Store the tarts in the refrigerator for up to 3 days. They're best served chilled.

Lemon curd tarts are a refreshing and elegant dessert with a bright lemon flavor that's sure to impress. Enjoy them at your next gathering or as a special treat!

Sweet Potato Fries

Ingredients:

- 2 large sweet potatoes
- 2 tablespoons olive oil
- 1 teaspoon paprika
- 1/2 teaspoon garlic powder
- 1/2 teaspoon onion powder
- 1/2 teaspoon ground cumin
- 1/4 teaspoon ground black pepper
- 1/2 teaspoon salt
- 1/4 teaspoon cayenne pepper (optional, for extra heat)

Instructions:

1. **Prepare the Sweet Potatoes:**
   - Preheat your oven to 425°F (220°C).
   - Peel the sweet potatoes and cut them into fry shapes, about 1/4 to 1/2 inch (0.6 to 1.3 cm) thick. Try to keep them as uniform in size as possible for even cooking.
2. **Season the Fries:**
   - In a large bowl, toss the sweet potato fries with the olive oil until they are well coated.
   - Add the paprika, garlic powder, onion powder, ground cumin, black pepper, salt, and cayenne pepper (if using). Toss again to ensure the spices are evenly distributed.
3. **Arrange for Baking:**
   - Line a baking sheet with parchment paper or a silicone baking mat for easy cleanup.
   - Spread the sweet potato fries out in a single layer on the baking sheet. Make sure they are not overcrowded; this helps them get crispy. If needed, use two baking sheets or bake in batches.
4. **Bake the Fries:**
   - Bake in the preheated oven for 20 minutes. After 20 minutes, flip the fries using a spatula to ensure even cooking.
   - Continue baking for an additional 15-20 minutes, or until the fries are crispy and golden brown. Baking times may vary depending on the thickness of the fries and your oven.
5. **Serve:**
   - Remove the fries from the oven and let them cool for a few minutes. They will crisp up a bit more as they cool.

- Serve with your favorite dipping sauces, such as ketchup, aioli, or a spicy mayo.

Tips:

- **Soaking:** For extra crispiness, soak the cut sweet potato fries in cold water for at least 30 minutes before baking. This helps remove excess starch. Be sure to pat them dry thoroughly before seasoning and baking.
- **Uniform Sizing:** Cutting the fries into uniform sizes ensures even cooking and helps achieve a consistent texture.
- **Avoid Overcrowding:** Spread the fries out in a single layer with space between them. Overcrowding can cause them to steam rather than crisp up.

Sweet potato fries are a versatile side dish or snack that pairs well with a variety of meals. Enjoy making and savoring your homemade crispy sweet potato fries!

www.ingramcontent.com/pod-product-compliance
Lightning Source LLC
LaVergne TN
LVHW081557060526
838201LV00054B/1943